More

QUICK ROTARY CUTTER

QUILTS

Pam Bono Designs

Oxmoor House®

More Quick Rotary Cutter Quilts
from the *For the Love of Quilting* series
©1996 by Oxmoor House, Inc.
Book Division of Southern Progress Corporation
P.O. Box 2463, Birmingham, Alabama 35201

Published by Oxmoor House, Inc., and
Leisure Arts, Inc.

Library of Congress Catalog Card
  Number: 95-72637
Hardcover ISBN: 0-8487-1512-8
Softcover ISBN: 0-8487-1514-4
Manufactured in the United States of America
Fifth Printing 1998

Editor-in-Chief: Nancy Fitzpatrick Wyatt
Senior Crafts Editor: Susan Ramey Cleveland
Senior Editor, Editorial Services: Olivia K. Wells
Art Director: James Boone

More Quick Rotary Cutter Quilts
Editor: Patricia Wilens
Copy Editor: Susan S. Cheatham
Editorial Assistant: Wendy Wolford Noah
Associate Art Director: Cynthia R. Cooper
Designer: Clare T. Minges
Illustrator: Karen Tindall Tillery
Senior Photographer: John O'Hagan
Photo Stylist: Katie Stoddard
Production and Distribution Director:
  Phillip Lee
Associate Production Manager:
  Theresa L. Beste
Production Assistant: Valerie L. Heard

Where to write to us: For billing, shipping, and other business inquiries, write to Oxmoor House Customer Service, P.O. Box 2463, Birmingham, AL 35201. If you have a question or comment regarding the content of this book, please write to Rotary Cutter Quilts, Oxmoor House, P.O. Box 2262, Birmingham, AL 35201.

This book is dedicated to our design partner, Mindy Kettner. Because of your exceptional design talents, this book is a real team effort. Thank you for bringing your great sense of humor into our lives. Mindy, this one's for you.

Introduction

Rotary cutting and quick piecing can change quiltmaking from plain labor to a labor of love. For us, these innovations make quilting fast (relatively speaking) and fun. The labor becomes a joyful, creative process; and when the work is done, our reward is to see our creation warm the hearts and hands of people we love.

We hear nice comments from quilters who discovered speed cutting and piecing in our first book, *Quick Rotary Cutter Quilts.* We love to hear someone say that these techniques opened doors, bringing fresh joy to an old pastime.

This book applies the same techniques to new designs, producing results that will please the most particular quilter. Beginners learn quick tricks that lead to beautiful quilts in much less time than traditional methods.

Basics and Beyond introduces each technique in detail, with step-by-step photos. If you are just learning these techniques, practice before beginning a project. This new type of patchwork may seem awkward at first, but you'll be comfortable and proficient in no time.

Also read **How to Use These Instructions** (page 26), which precedes the quilt instructions. This explains how instructions are formatted and some rules of thumb that apply throughout.

We hope you find as much pleasure in making these quilts as we did designing them for you. Happy quilting!

Pam Bono   Robert Bono

Pam Bono Designs

Contents

Basics and Beyond

46

12

52

Rotary Cutter Quilt Collection

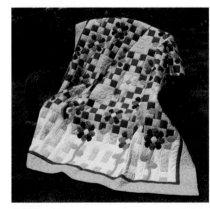

120

146

141

Basics and Beyond

Fabric

Lightweight, 100%-cotton fabric is the best choice for quilts. Sturdy and durable, cotton is neither stretchy nor tightly woven and it takes a crease well, so seams are easy to press. When you use good-quality fabric, your quilt looks nice and lasts a long time.

Selecting Fabric

Choosing fabrics seems to bring out the insecurities in many quilt-makers. Will my quilt look as good as the one in the picture? If I change the color to blue, will my quilt look as nice as the green one?

Trust Your Instincts. Go with the fabrics *you* like. You can ask for help from family, friends, and helpful shop staff, but the final choice is yours.

We exhaust the people at our favorite quilt shops. We'll take down half the bolts in the store to try different combinations. We put our choices together on a large table and then—this is very impor-tant—step back and *squint*. This lets us preview the mix of value and texture. If one fabric doesn't blend, we'll replace it and try again. And again. And again, until we're satisfied.

Prewashing

Wash, dry, and iron all fabrics before cutting. Use the same washer and detergent that you'll use to wash the finished quilt, so you won't get any rude surprises later. Washing removes excess dye and sizing from the fabric and may shrink it slightly. If you take the time to prewash, there's less chance of damage occurring later.

Wash light and dark colors sepa-rately in warm water. Use a mild detergent or Orvus Paste, a mild soap available at many quilt shops.

Test for Colorfastness. You want to be sure to get out excess dye before you use the fabric. After washing, rinse each piece in the sink, adding a clean scrap of white fabric. If the scrap gets stained, rinse again. Continue until the scrap remains white. If repeated rinsing doesn't stop the bleeding, don't use that fabric—take it back to the store where you bought it and *complain!*

Dry and Press. Dry prewashed fabrics at a medium or permanent-press setting in the dryer until they're just damp. Then press them dry. It's important to iron out all the creases and folds so you'll have smooth, straight fabric with which to work.

Grain Lines

The interwoven lengthwise and crosswise threads of a fabric are grain lines. The following are some things to know about grain before you cut. Cotton fabric can be stable or stretchy, depending on how it is cut.

Selvage. The lengthwise finished edges of the fabric are selvages (Grain Diagram). These edges are more tightly woven than the body of the fabric and are sometimes not printed. *Always trim selvage from the ends of a strip before cutting pieces for your quilt.*

Straight Grain. Lengthwise grain, parallel to the selvage, has the least give. Long strips for sashing and borders are best cut lengthwise for more stability.

Crosswise grain, perpendicular to the selvage, has a little more give. Most strips are cut on the crosswise grain. For small patchwork pieces, either direction is acceptable.

Bias. True bias is at a 45° angle to the selvages, on the diagonal between lengthwise and crosswise grains (Grain Diagram).

Bias-cut fabric has the most stretch. When you cut a triangle, at least one edge is bias. Handle a bias edge carefully, as it can stretch out of shape, warping the patchwork.

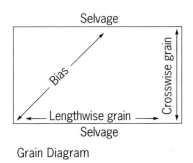

Grain Diagram

Rotary Cutting

Rotary cutting is fast and easy. It's fast because you measure and cut with one stroke. It's accurate because the fabric stays flat as you cut, instead of being raised by a scissor blade. If rotary cutting is new to you, use these instructions to practice on scraps. It may seem strange at first, but try it—you'll love it!

Get Equipped

Rotary cutters, cutting mats, and cutting rulers come in many sizes and styles. Choose a cutter that is comfortable to hold. Change the blade often.

The most useful cutting mat is 24" x 36", but I have a smaller one for cutting scraps.

Rulers. Rotary-cutting rulers are thick transparent acrylic. Select rulers that are marked in increments of 1", ¼", and ⅛". A 45°-angle line is also useful.

The rulers I use most are a 6" x 24" for cutting long strips, a 15" square, and a 6" x 12".

Squaring Up the Edge

Fabric off the bolt is likely to have jagged edges or be folded off-center. Prewashing the fabric should eliminate the crease of the fold. To cut straight strips, you should refold the fabric and square up the ends.

1. Fold the fabric with selvages matching. Place the fabric on a cutting mat with the fold nearest you.

Then fold the fabric in half again, bringing the selvages down almost even with the fold to make four layers (Photo A). The yardage extends to your right, leaving the end you are cutting on the mat. (Reverse directions if you are left-handed.)

2. Align the bottom of a large square ruler with the bottom fold so the left edge of the ruler is 1" from the end of the fabric (Photo B). Butt a long ruler against the left side of the square, overlapping the fabric edge. Keeping the long ruler in place, remove the square.

3. Release the safety guard on the cutter. Keeping the ruler stable with your left hand, hold the cutter blade against the ruler at the bottom of the mat. Begin rolling the cutter before it meets the fabric, moving the cutter away from you (Photo C).

Keep the ruler stable and the blade against the ruler. Do not lift the cutter until it cuts through the opposite edge of the fabric.

First Cut

Rotary cutting often begins with cutting strips of fabric, which are then cut into smaller pieces. In this book, instructions for the first cut (designated by ✻), specify the number and width of strips needed. Unless specified otherwise, cut strips crosswise, selvage to selvage.

Instructions for the second cut (designated by •) state the quantity, size, and unit number of the pieces to cut from these strips. *Seam allowances are included in measurements for all strips and pieces.*

1. To measure the strip width, position the ruler on the left edge of the fabric. Carefully align the desired measurement with the edge, checking the line on the ruler from top to bottom of the fabric. Cut, holding the ruler firmly in place (Photo D). A sharp blade cuts easily through all four layers.

2. Examine the cut strip. If the edge of the fabric is not squared up properly, the strip will bow in the middle (Photo E, top). Square up the edge again and cut another strip.

3. Rotary-cut ½" from the strip ends to remove selvages.

Second Cut

To cut squares and rectangles from a strip, align the desired measurement on the ruler with the end of the strip and cut across the strip (Photo F).

For right triangles, instructions may say to cut a square in half or in quarters diagonally (Photo G). This works with rectangles, too. The edges of the square or rectangle are straight grain, so diagonal edge of the triangle is bias. On these pieces, run a line of stay-stitching ⅛" from the bias edge to keep the fabric from stretching as you work with it.

Organize Cut Pieces

It's easy to get cut pieces mixed up unless they are neatly stored and organized—especially if, like many people, you are constantly moving your work on and off the dining room table. It's important to be sure which piece is which when you've cut so many.

I place all my cut pieces in a zip-top plastic bag, labelled with the unit number (Photo H). You can see the fabric through the bag, which helps you locate pieces as you work. If the sewing takes several weeks, the pieces inside the bags don't get lost, mixed up, or dirty. Keep the bags close to your sewing machine for easy access and remove one piece at a time as you work.

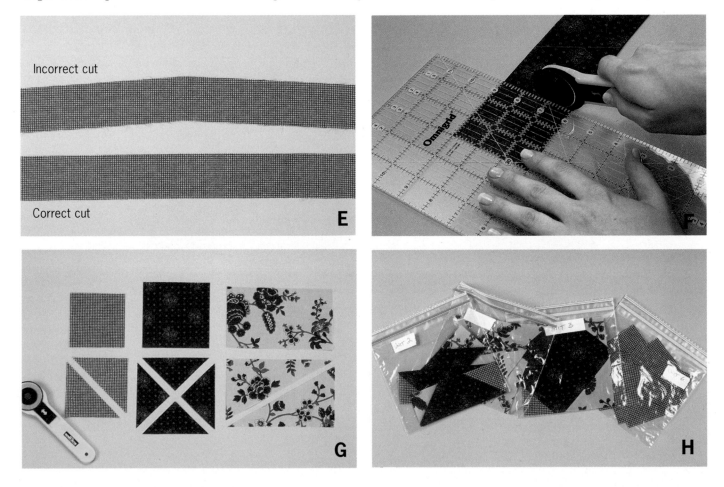

Incorrect cut

Correct cut

E

F

G

H

Machine Piecing

An accurate, consistent ¼" seam allowance is essential for good patchwork. If each seam varies by the tiniest bit, the difference multiplies greatly by the time a block is complete. Before you start a project, be sure your machine is in good order and that you can sew a precise ¼" seam allowance.

Measure the Seam

On some sewing machines, you can adjust the needle position to make a ¼" seam. If your needle is not adjustable, use a presser foot that is ¼" from the needle to the outside edge of the foot. These feet are available at sewing supply stores.

Make a Seam Guide. Another way to gauge a seam is to mark the throat plate. Use a sharp pencil with a ruler to draw a line ¼" from the edge of a piece of paper. Lower the machine needle onto the line, drop the foot, and adjust the paper to parallel the foot (Photo A). Lay masking tape on the throat plate at the edge of the paper.

Sew a seam, using the guide. Check the seam allowance—if it gets wider or narrower, the tape is not straight. Adjust the tape as needed until the seam is accurate.

Machine Stitching

Set your sewing machine to 12–14 stitches per inch. Use 100%-cotton or cotton/polyester sewing thread.

Match pieces to be sewn with right sides facing. Sew each seam from cut edge to cut edge of the fabric piece. It is not necessary to backstitch, because most seams will be crossed and held by another.

To piece a block, join small pieces first to form units. Then join units to form larger ones until the block is complete. (See assembly diagrams with quilt instructions.)

Sew an X. When triangles are pieced with other units, seams should cross in an X on the back. If the joining seam goes precisely through the center of the X (Photo B), the triangle will have a nice sharp point on the front.

Press and Pin

To make neat corners and points, seams must meet precisely. Pressing and pinning can help achieve matched seams.

To press, set your iron for cotton. Use an up-and-down motion, lifting the iron from spot to spot. Sliding the iron back and forth can push seams out of shape. First press the seam flat on the wrong side; then open the piece and press the right side.

Press to One Side. Press patchwork seam allowances to one side, not open as in dressmaking. If possible, press toward the darker fabric to avoid seam allowances showing through light fabrics.

Press seam allowances in opposite directions from row to row (Photo C). By offsetting seam allowances at each intersection, you reduce the bulk under the patchwork. This is more important than whether seam allowances are pressed toward dark or light.

Pin Matching. Use pins to match seam lines. With right sides facing, align opposing seams, nesting seam allowances. On the top piece, push

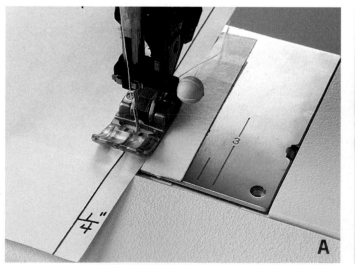

a pin through the seam line ¼" from the edge (Photo D). Then push the pin through the bottom seam and set it. Pin all matching seams; then stitch the joining seam, removing pins as you sew.

Easing Fullness

Sometimes two units that should be the same size are slightly different. When joining such units, pin-match opposing seams. Sew the seam with the shorter piece on top (Easing Diagram). As you sew, the feed dogs ease the fullness on the bottom piece. This is called sewing "with a baggy bottom."

If units are too dissimilar to ease without puckering, check each one to see if the pieces were correctly cut and that the seams are ¼" wide. Remake the unit that varies most from the desired size.

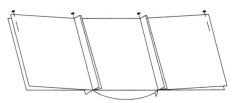

Easing Diagram

Chain Piecing

Chain piecing is an efficient way to sew many units in one operation, saving time and thread.

Line up several units to be sewn. Sew the first unit as usual, but at the end of the seam do not back-stitch, clip the thread, or lift the presser foot. Instead, feed in the next unit right on the heels of the first. There will be a little twist of thread between units (Photo E).

Sew as many seams as you like on a chain. Keep the chain intact to carry it to the ironing board and clip the threads as you press.

Quick-Piecing Techniques

You can make any quilt in this book using the methods explained here. These methods are uniquely suited to machine sewing. Combined with rotary cutting, they reduce cutting and sewing time without sacrificing results.

Strip Piecing

For some projects, you'll join strips of different fabrics to make what is called a strip set. Project directions specify how to cut strips and each strip set is illustrated.

To sew a strip set, match each pair of strips with right sides facing. Stitch through both layers along one long edge (Photo A). When sewing multiple strips in a set, practice "anti-directional" stitching to keep strips straight. As you add strips, sew each new seam in the *opposite* direction from the last one (Diagram 1). This distributes tension evenly in both directions and keeps the strip set from getting warped and wobbly.

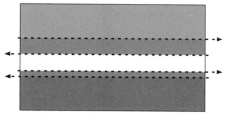

Diagram 1

Cut Segments. After a strip set is assembled and pressed, you will cut it into segments. Use a ruler to measure; then make appropriate crosswise cuts to get individual segments (Photo B). Each segment becomes a unit in the design.

This technique is fast and accurate because you assemble and press a unit *before* it is cut from the strip set.

Diagonal Corners

This technique turns squares into sewn triangles with just a stitch and a snip. It is particularly helpful if the corner triangle is very small, because it's easier to cut and handle a square than a small triangle. By sewing squares to squares, you don't have to guess where seam allowances meet, which can be difficult with triangles. The ease and speed with which you'll sew these corners is delightful.

Project instructions give the size of the fabric pieces needed. The

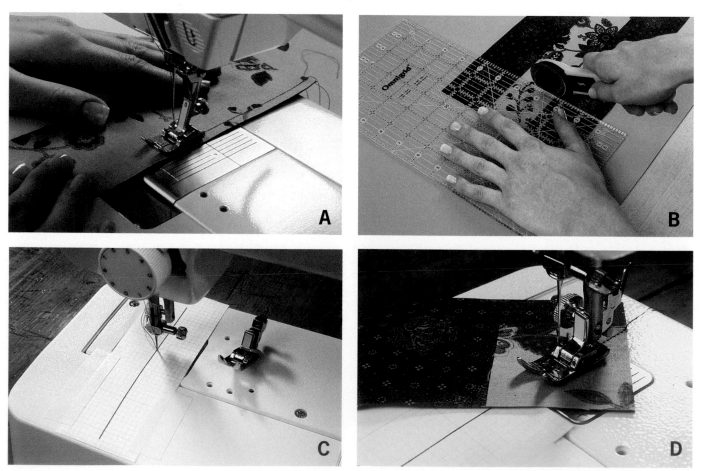

base fabric is either a square or a rectangle, but the contrasting corner always starts out as a square.

Make a Seam Guide. Before sewing, make a seam guide that will enable you to machine-stitch diagonal lines without having to mark the fabric beforehand.

Draw a 5"-long line on graph paper. Place the paper on the sewing machine and bring the needle down through the line (Photo C). Remove the foot if necessary for a good viewpoint. Use a ruler to verify that the line is parallel to the needle. Tape the paper to the throat plate. Trim the top edge of the paper to leave the needle and presser foot unobstructed.

1. With right sides facing, match the small square to one corner of the base fabric.

2. Align the top tip of the small square with the needle and the bottom tip with the seam guide. Stitch a seam from tip to tip, keeping the

bottom tip of the square in line with the seam guide (Photo D).

3. Press the small square in half at the seam (Photo E).

4. Trim the seam allowance to ¼" (Photo F).

Repeat the procedure to add a diagonal corner to two, three, or four corners of the base fabric.

This technique is the same when you add a diagonal corner to a strip set or a diagonal end—treat the base fabric as one piece, even if it is already pieced.

When sewing a large diagonal corner, draw or press a stitching line through the center of the corner square.

Diagonal Ends

This method joins two rectangles on the diagonal and eliminates the difficulty of measuring and cutting a trapezoid. It is similar to the diagonal-corner technique, but

here you work with two rectangles. Project instructions specify the size of each rectangle.

To sew diagonal ends, make a seam guide for your machine as described for diagonal corners.

1. Place rectangles perpendicular to each other with right sides facing, matching corners to be sewn.

2. Before you sew, pin on the stitching line and check the right side to see if the line is angled in the desired direction.

3. Position the rectangles under the needle, leading with the top edge. Sew a diagonal seam to the opposite edge (Photo G).

4. Check the right side to see that the seam is angled correctly. Then press the seam and trim excess fabric from the seam allowance.

5. As noted in Step 2, the direction of the seam makes a difference (Photo H). Make mirror-image units with this in mind, or you can put different ends on the same strip.

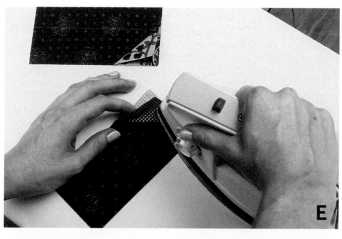

E

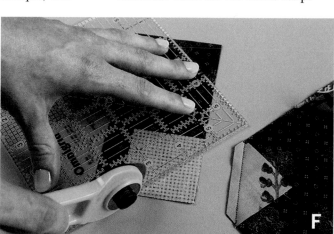

F

G

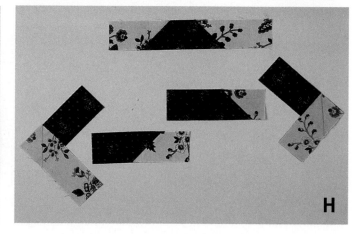

H

Quick-Pieced Triangles

The triangle is a basic element of patchwork. But cutting and sewing triangles pose unique problems for quilters. These quick-piecing techniques eliminate those difficulties and enable you to create many pre-sewn units with one process—a real time-saver when you're making a large quilt.

Triangle-Squares

Many patchwork designs are made by joining two contrasting triangles to make a square. I use the grid method of sewing triangle-squares. In these projects, instructions describe a grid that is the basis for making a lot of triangle-squares quickly and easily.

Cutting instructions specify two fabric squares or rectangles for each grid. Spray both pieces with spray starch to keep the fabric from distorting during marking and stitching. Accuracy is important in every step—if your marking, cutting, sewing, and pressing are not precise, your triangle-squares may be lopsided or the wrong size.

Marking the Grid. For marking, use a see-through ruler and a fine-tipped fabric pen—a pencil drags on the fabric, making an inaccurate line and stretching the fabric.

1. Let's say, for example, instructions call for a 2 x 4 grid of 2⅛" squares. This describes a grid of eight squares, drawn two down and four across (Diagram 1). Draw the grid on the *wrong* side of the lighter fabric. The fabric size allows a margin of at least 1" around the grid, so align the ruler parallel to one side of the fabric, 1" from the edge, and draw the first line.

2. Draw the second line exactly 2⅛" from the first. Continue in this manner, using the ruler's markings to position each new line. Take care to make lines accurately parallel and/or perpendicular—the size and shape of your triangle-squares depend on it.

3. When the grid is complete, draw a diagonal line through each square (Diagram 2). Alternate direction of diagonals in adjacent squares.

Stitching the Grid. With right sides facing, match all edges of the two fabric pieces.

1. Start at an outside point near the top left corner of the grid (blue arrow, Diagram 3).

2. Sewing a ¼" seam allowance, stitch alongside the diagonals

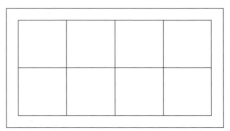

Diagram 1

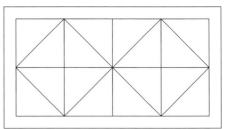

Diagram 2

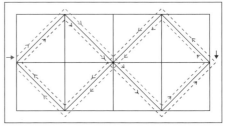

Diagram 3

indicated by the blue line. At the end of one line, stitch into the margin as shown. Keep the needle down, but raise the foot and pivot the fabric so you can stitch along the next line. When you return to the starting point, you'll have stitched on one side of all diagonal lines.

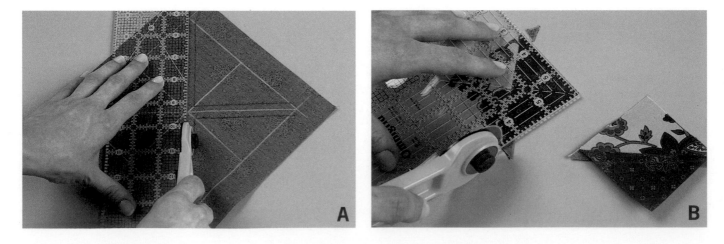

3. Begin again at another outside point (red arrow on sample grid). Repeat stitching on the opposite side of the diagonal lines.

    Cutting and Pressing. When the grid is completely stitched, press the fabric to smooth the stitching.

1. Rotary-cut on *all* the drawn lines to separate the triangle-squares (Photo A). Each grid square yields two triangle-squares, so our previous example would produce 16 units.

2. Press each triangle-square open, pressing the seam allowance toward the darker fabric.

3. Trim points from ends of each seam allowance (Photo B).

    In our example, we're working toward a desired finished size of 1¼" square. The grid squares are drawn ⅞" larger than the finished size. After the grid is sewn, the cut and pressed square is ½" larger than the finished size (1¾").

Four-Triangle Squares

You can quick-piece squares made of four triangles using an expanded version of the grid method above that produces two-triangle squares. Marking and stitching the grid is the same, except that you start with grid squares 1¼" larger than the desired finished size.

    Project instructions specify how to mark and sew a grid and how many triangle-squares will result.

1. On the wrong side of one triangle-square, draw a diagonal line through the center, bisecting the seam (Photo C).

2. Match the marked square with another triangle-square, with right sides facing. Position the squares with *contrasting* fabrics together (Photo D).

3. Stitch ¼" seam on both sides of the drawn diagonal line (Photo E).

4. Cut units apart on the drawn line (Photo F). Press units open and trim points from seam allowances.

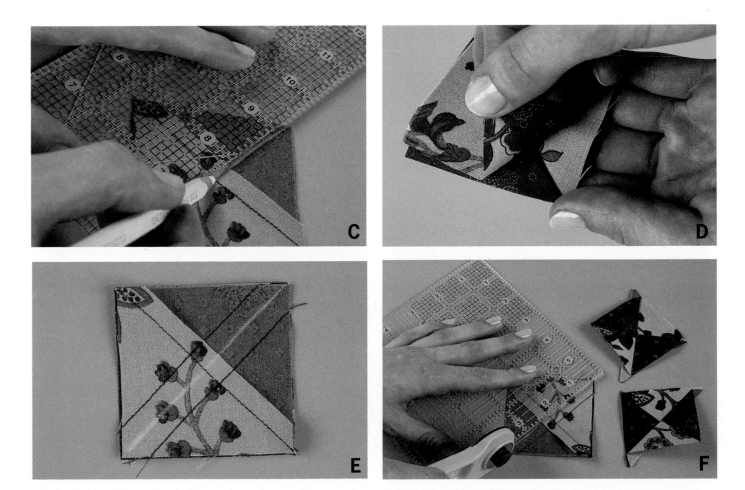

Joining Blocks

The easiest way to join blocks is in rows, either diagonally, vertically, or horizontally. All the quilts in this book are pieced in this manner.

Sew by the Row

Arrange blocks on the floor or a large table. Identify the pieces in each row and verify the position of each block. This is play time—moving the blocks around to find the best balance of color and value is great fun. Don't start sewing until you're happy with the placement of each block.

Pin-match. As you join blocks in each row, pick up one block at a time to avoid confusion. Pin-match adjoining seams. Re-press a seam if necessary to offset seam allowances. If some blocks are larger than others, pinning may help determine where easing is required. A blast of steam from the iron may help fit the blocks together.

Pressing. When a row is assembled, press seam allowances between blocks in the same direction. For the next row, press seam allowances in the opposite direction (Diagram 1).

In an alternate set, straight or diagonal, press seam allowances between blocks toward setting squares or triangles (Diagram 2). This creates the least bulk and always results in opposing seam allowances when adjacent rows are joined.

Sashing eliminates cares about opposing seam allowances. Assemble horizontal rows with sashing strips between blocks; then press the new seam allowances toward the sashing (Diagram 3). If necessary, ease the block to match the length of the sashing strip. Assemble the quilt top with rows of sashing between block rows, always pressing seam allowances toward the sashing strips.

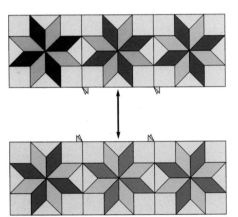

Diagram 1

Diagram 2

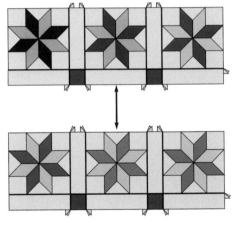

Diagram 3

Mail-Order Resources

Pam Bono Designs offers The Angler™—a sewing guide for the quick-piecing techniques described in this book. Easy to use with any sewing machine. For information on this and other products, contact *Pam Bono Designs* at P.O. Box 5355, Durango, CO 81301 or telephone 970-259-5426.

Quiltmaking supplies are available at many craft and fabric stores, especially quilting specialty shops. Consult your local telephone directory to find a shop in your area.

If you prefer to have things delivered to your door, order supplies from a mail-order source. These catalogs are good suppliers of fabric, batting, stencils, notions, and other quilting supplies. Both have toll-free telephone numbers and will mail you a catalog at no charge.

Keepsake Quilting
P.O. Box 1618
Centre Harbor, NH 03226
(800) 865-9458

Connecting Threads
P.O. Box 8940
Vancouver, WA 98668-8940
(800) 574-6454

Borders

Most quilts have one wide border or several narrow ones that frame the design. In this book, all quilts are made with square corners. Before you sew, measure the quilt and trim border strips to fit properly.

Measuring

It's common for one side of a quilt top to be a slightly different measurement than its opposite side. No matter how careful your piecing, tiny variables add up. You want to sew borders of equal length to opposite sides to square up the quilt.

Cutting instructions for borders include extra length to allow for piecing variations.

1. Measure the quilt from top to bottom *through the middle* of the quilt (Photo A). (For a large quilt, use a 10-foot measuring tape.) Trim both side border strips to this measurement. Sew borders to quilt sides, easing as needed.

2. For top and bottom borders, measure from side to side through the middle of the quilt (Photo B). Trim and sew borders as before.

This example joins side borders first, and then top and bottom borders. Sometimes it is practical to reverse the sequence. Instructions specify the order in which you should sew borders.

Contrasting Corners

If you plan to add a contrasting corner, measure and trim all four borders *before* sewing side borders to quilt. Stitch a contrasting block to the ends of the top and bottom border strips. When sewn to the quilt, the seams of the blocks should align with the side border seams.

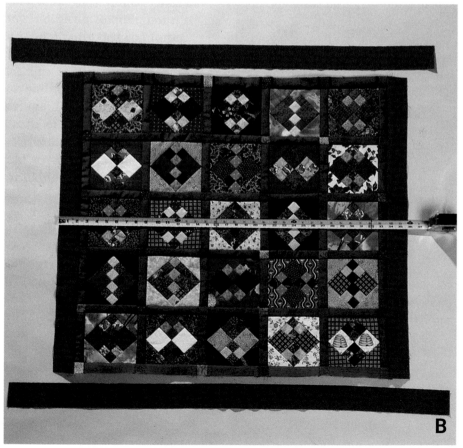

Binding

These instructions are for double-fold straight-grain binding. Doubled binding is stronger than one layer, so it better protects the edges, where a quilt suffers the most wear. We like straight-grain binding because it is easier to make than bias binding and requires less fabric.

Making Continuous Binding

Each project specifies the number of cross-grain strips to cut for binding. Cut 3" wide, these strips result in a finished binding ½"–⅝" wide. Make wider binding when using thick batting.

To join two strips end-to-end, match the ends perpendicular to each other with right sides facing. Stitch a diagonal seam across the corner (Photo A). Trim seam allowances to ¼" and press them open.

Join strips end-to-end in this manner to make one continuous strip that is the length specified in the project instructions.

Applying Binding

1. With wrong sides facing, press the binding in half along the length of the strip (Photo B).

2. With raw edges aligned, position the binding on the front of the quilt top, in the middle of any side. Leave 3" of binding free before the point where you begin (Photo C).
3. Stitch through all layers with a ¼" seam. Stop stitching ¼" from the quilt corner and backstitch (Photo D). (Placing a pin at the ¼" point beforehand will show you where to stop.) Remove the quilt from the machine.
4. Rotate the quilt a quarter turn. Fold the binding straight up, away from the corner, and make a 45°-angle fold (Photo E).
5. Bring the binding straight down in line with the next edge, leaving the top fold even with the raw edge

of the previously sewn side. Begin stitching at the top edge, sewing through all layers (Photo F). Stitch all corners in this manner.

6. Stop stitching as you approach the beginning point. Fold the 3" tail of binding over on itself and pin (Photo G). The end of the binding will overlap this folded section. Continue stitching through all layers to 1" beyond the folded tail. Trim any extra binding.

7. Trim the batting and backing nearly even with the seam allowance, leaving a little extra to fill out the binding.

8. Fold the binding over the seam allowance to the back. When turned, the beginning fold conceals the raw end of the binding (Photo H).

9. Blindstitch the folded edge of the binding to the backing fabric (Photo I). Fold a miter into the binding at back corners.

E

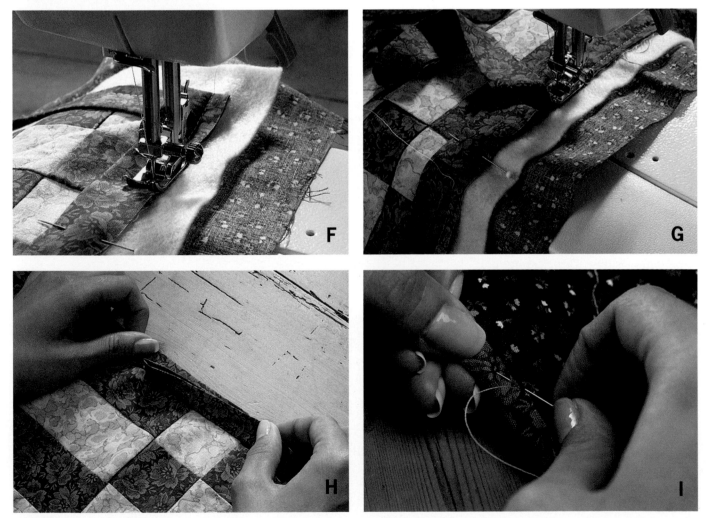

F

G

H

I

Care and Cleaning

A quilt's greatest enemies are light and dirt. To keep your quilt in prime condition would mean never using it. But then you'd never get to see it, enjoy it, or share it. Your quilt can last a lifetime if you treat it with care.

Safekeeping

A quilt is bound to fade over time. But you can reduce the risks by keeping the quilt away from strong sunlight and storing it properly when not in use.

Alternate your quilts every few months to reduce exposure. Store an unused quilt—with as few folds as possible—in a cotton pillowcase. Don't use plastic bags, which trap moisture. To prevent permanent creases, stored quilts should occasionally be aired and refolded. Wads of acid-free paper inside the folds also discourage creases.

Washing

Wash quilts infrequently. A good airing is usually all that's needed to freshen a quilt. Vacuuming with a hose removes dust. Dry cleaning is bad for quilts because it leaves harmful chemicals in the fabric.

When you must wash a quilt, use a mild soap such as Ensure or Orvis Paste. These soaps (as well as acid-free paper) are available at quilt shops and from mail-order resources (see page 16).

A Good Soak. If fabrics are pre-washed, you can wash your quilt in the washing machine if the machine is large enough. Wash an extra-large quilt in the bathtub, letting it soak in warm soapy water

for about 15 minutes. Rinse repeatedly to remove the soap.

Drying. Squeeze as much water out of the quilt as possible, but don't wring or twist it. Carefully lift the quilt out of the washer or tub, supporting its weight with your arms so that no part of the quilt is pulled or stressed. Place the quilt flat between two layers of towels, and roll it up to remove as much moisture as possible.

Putting a wet quilt in a dryer is not recommended, because heat and agitation can damage fabric and batting.

Dry a damp quilt flat on a floor or table. If you want to dry it outside, pick a shady spot on a sunny day, and place the quilt between sheets to protect it. When the quilt is almost dry, and if it isn't too large, you can put it in the dryer on a cool setting to smooth out wrinkles and fluff it up.

Hanging

If you want to hang your quilt on a wall, make a hanging sleeve as described on page 130. Do not use pushpins or tacks to hang a quilt, because the metal can leave rust stains on the fabric. Also, the weight of the quilt pulls against the pins, distorting the edge of the quilt and damaging the fibers.

Measuring Metric and Computing Fractions

If you are accustomed to the metric system, this chart will be helpful in establishing conversions for common measurements. Or, if you are buying fabric in the U.S.A., use the decimals column and your calculator to figure cost. For example, if you're buying 1⅜ yards of $8.50-a-yard fabric, multiply $8.50 by 1.375 to get a cost of $11.69.

Inches	Fractions	Decimals	Meters
¼"	.25"	.635 cm	
½"	.5"	1.27 cm	
¾"	.75"	1.91 cm	
1"	1.0"	2.54 cm	
4½"	⅛ yard	.125 yard	11.43 cm
9"	¼ yard	.25 yard	22.86 cm
13½"	⅜ yard	.375 yard	.3375 m
18"	½ yard	.5 yard	.45 m
22½"	⅝ yard	.625 yard	.563 m
27"	¾ yard	.75 yard	.675 m
31½"	⅞ yard	.875 yard	.788 m
36"	1 yard	1 yard	.9 m
39⅜"	1 1/10 yards	1.1 yards	1 m

When you know:	Multiply by:	To find:
inches	2.54	centimeters (cm)
yards	.9	meters (m)

GREYSCALE

BIN TRAVELER FORM

Cut By_____Y.B_____ Qty _39___ Date_____

Scanned By_____ Qty_____ Date_____

Scanned Batch IDs

_____   _____   _____

Notes / Exception

_____

_____

_____

_____

_____

ROTARY CUTTER QUILT
COLLECTION

How to Use These Instructions

The following notes explain how these instructions are organized. You'll find the quiltmaking easier if you keep these tips in mind.

✱ At the beginning of each project, you'll find a list of quick-piecing techniques used to make that quilt. Before beginning the project, see *Basics and Beyond* for general instructions on each technique.

✱ A color key accompanies each materials list, matching each fabric with the color-coded illustrations given with the project directions.

✱ Cutting instructions are given for each fabric. The first cut, indicated by a ✱, is usually a specified number of crossgrain strips.

✱ Second cuts, indicated by a •, specify how to cut those strips into smaller pieces. The identification of each piece follows in parentheses, consisting of the block letter and unit number that correspond to the assembly diagrams. For pieces used in more than one unit, several unit numbers may be given.

✱ Organize cut pieces in zip-top bags and label each bag with the appropriate unit numbers. This avoids confusion and keeps a lot of pieces stored safely until they're needed.

✱ Large pieces such as sashings and borders are usually cut first to be sure you have enough fabric.

✱ To reduce waste, you may be instructed to cut some pieces from a first-cut strip and then cut that strip down to a narrower width to cut additional pieces.

✱ Cutting lists identify triangle-square units in the same way as for other pieces, but the piece cut is large enough to sew a grid as directed in the project instructions. Each piece allows a margin of 1" of fabric around the grid.

✱ Cutting instructions are given for the whole quilt as shown. If you want to make just one block, see information at right.

✱ Cutting and piecing instructions are given in a logical step-by-step progression. Follow this order in all cases to avoid confusion.

✱ Every project has one or more block designs. Instructions include block illustrations that show the fabric colors and the numbered units.

✱ Individual units are assembled first, using one or more of the quick-piecing techniques described in *Basics and Beyond*.

✱ Strip-set illustrations show the size of the segments to be cut from that strip set. The unit number of the segment is also shown. Keep strip-set segments in a labelled zip-top bag as for other units.

✱ An assembly diagram is given for each block. Each numbered unit is isolated, with + symbols indicating how units are joined. Follow the instructions to join units in the proper sequence. Some blocks are further divided into sections, which are joined according to instructions.

Rules of Thumb

Here are a few things to keep in mind when making the quilts in this collection. For more detailed quilt-making information, turn to the *Basics and Beyond* chapter, which begins on page 6.

✱ Yardages are based on 45"-wide fabric, allowing for up to 4% shrinkage.

✱ Materials are listed to make each quilt as shown. Select similar fabrics or fabrics in the colors of your choice in the quantities stated.

✱ 100% cotton fabric is recommended for the quilt top and for backing. Wash, dry, and press fabrics before cutting.

✱ Read all instructions for the selected project before you begin to cut.

✱ Cut pieces from each fabric in the order in which they are listed, cutting largest pieces first. This ensures efficient use of yardage.

✱ All seam allowances are ¼". Seam allowances are included in all stated measurements and cutting instructions.

✱ Store cut pieces in labelled zip-top bags.

✱ The quilts in this book can be made in a relatively short time because of the methods used. But remember than everyone works at his or her own speed—don't feel like you're racing the clock to get your quilt finished. Relax and enjoy the creative process.

✱ Each unit in the assembly diagram is numbered. The main part of the unit is indicated with the number only. A diagonal line represents a seam where a diagonal corner or end is attached. Each diagonal piece is numbered with the main unit number plus a letter (such as 1a).

✱ Some units have multiple diagonal corners or ends. When these are the same size and are cut from the same fabric, the identifying letter is the same. But if the unit has multiple diagonal pieces that are different in size and/or color, the letters are different. These pieces are joined to the main unit in alphabetical order.

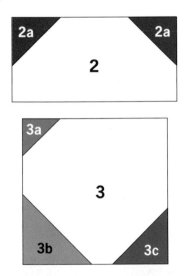

✱ Triangle-squares are shown as assembled, with the unit number in the center of the square.

✱ Practice the quick-cutting and quick-piecing methods with scrap fabrics before beginning a project. Refer to assembly diagrams frequently, following the unit identification system carefully. Organizing your work as suggested will save time and avoid confusion.

✱ Piecing instructions are given for making one block. Make the number of blocks stated in the project instructions to complete the project as shown.

How to Make One Block

Cutting instructions are given for making the quilt as shown. But sometimes you want to make just one block for a project of your own design. What then?

All you have to do is count. Or divide, if you prefer.

With each cutting list is an illustration of the block(s). The unit numbers in the cutting list correspond to the units in the illustration. Count how many of each unit are in the block illustration. Instead of cutting the number shown in the cutting list, cut the number you need for one block.

If you prefer, you can figure it out just from the cutting list. If the quilt shown has 20 blocks, for example, then divide each quantity by 20 to determine how many pieces are needed for one block.

Chains of *Love*

The Irish Chain is a best-loved quilt design, and this one takes tradition to heart. Select a luscious floral print for the main fabric and then choose four more fabrics to coordinate.

Finished Size

Quilt: 82" x 110"
Blocks: 18 heart blocks, 14" square
17 chain blocks, 14" square

Quick-Piecing Techniques

Strip Piecing (see page 12)
Diagonal Corners (see page 12)

Materials

	Fabric I (dark plum large print)	2 yards
	Fabric II (green print)	1⅞ yards
	Fabric III (plum print or solid)	2¾ yards
	Fabric IV (pink print)	2¾ yards
	Fabric V (white-on-white print)	2⅜ yards
	Backing fabric	6½ yards
	Precut batting	90" x 108"

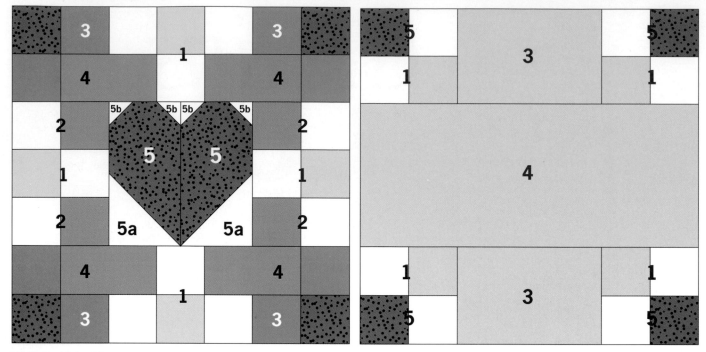

Block A—Make 18.

Block B—Make 17.

Cutting

Cut all strips crossgrain, from selvage to selvage. For best use of yardage, cut pieces in order listed. See diagrams to identify strip sets.

From Fabric I (dark plum), cut:

✷ Three 6½"-wide strips. From these, cut:
  • Thirty-six 3½" x 6½" (A5).
✷ Seventeen 2½"-wide strips. Set aside 10 strips for strip sets 3 and 5. From remaining strips, cut:
  • Six 2½" x 22½" (Border 2).
  • Four 2½" x 20½" (Border 3).
  • Four 2½" x 18½" (Border 1).

From Fabric II (green), cut:

✷ Twenty-four 2½"-wide strips. Set aside 10 strips for strip sets 3 and 4. From remaining strips, cut:
  • Fourteen 2½" x 26½" (Border 4).

From Fabric III (plum), cut:

✷ Five 4½"-wide strips for Strip Set 4.
✷ Fifteen 2½"-wide strips. Set aside five strips for Strip Set 2 and 10 strips for outer border.
✷ Ten 3"-wide strips for binding.

From Fabric IV (pink), cut:

✷ Ten 2½"-wide strips for strip sets 1 and 6.
✷ Ten 6½"-wide strips. From these, cut:
  • Seventeen 6½" x 14½" (B4).
  • Thirty-four 4½" x 6½" (B3).

From Fabric V (white), cut:

✷ Twenty-five 2½"-wide strips for strip sets 1, 2, 3, 5, and 6. From ends of 10 of these strips, cut:
  • Ten 2½" squares for middle border.
✷ Three 3½"-wide strips. From these, cut:
  • Thirty-six 3½" squares (A5a).
✷ Three 1½"-wide strips. From these, cut:
  • Seventy-two 1½" squares (A5b).

Units for Block A

Refer to strip set diagrams and Block A Assembly Diagram throughout to identify units. Store units cut from each strip set in labelled zip-top bags. In block assembly, unit numbers will be the same as strip set numbers.

1. For Strip Set 1, join strips of fabrics IV and V as shown. Make nine of Strip Set 1. Press seam allowances toward Fabric IV. From these strip sets, cut 140 2½"-wide segments for Unit 1.

2. For Strip Set 2, join strips of fabrics III and V as shown. Make five of Strip Set 2. Press seam allowances toward Fabric III. From these strip sets, cut seventy-two 2½"-wide segments for Unit 2.

3. For Strip Set 3, join strips of fabrics I, II, and V as shown. Make five of Strip Set 3. Press seam allowances toward Fabric II. From these strip sets, cut seventy-two 2½"-wide segments for Unit 3.

4. For Strip Set 4, join strips of fabrics II (2½"-wide) and III (4½"-wide) as shown. Make five of Strip Set 4. Press seam allowances toward Fabric II. From these strip sets, cut seventy-two 2½"-wide segments for Unit 4.

5. Use diagonal-corner technique to make two of Unit 5. These are mirror images, so be careful to position each 5a piece in opposite corners as shown.

Block A Assembly

Assemble this block in sections X, Y, and Z. Each completed section should measure approximately 14½" wide. Refer to Block A Assembly Diagram throughout.

Sections X and Z

1. For Section X, join two pair of units 3 and 4 as shown. Sew combined units to opposite sides of one Unit 1.

2. Repeat to make Section Z.

Section Y

1. Join mirror-image Unit 5s to make a heart.

2. Sew one of Unit 2 to opposite sides of Unit 1. Make two 2/1/2 units.

3. Join 2/1/2 units to opposite sides of heart unit.

Assembly

Join sections X, Y, and Z to complete block. Make 18 of Block A.

(continued)

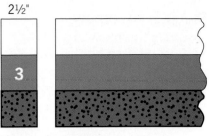

2½"

Strip Set 1—Make 9.

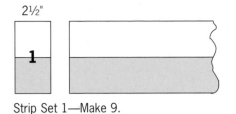

2½"

Strip Set 2—Make 5.

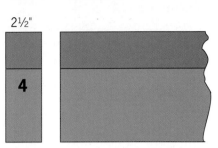

2½"

Strip Set 3—Make 5.

2½"

Strip Set 4—Make 5.

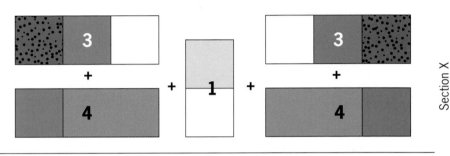
Section X

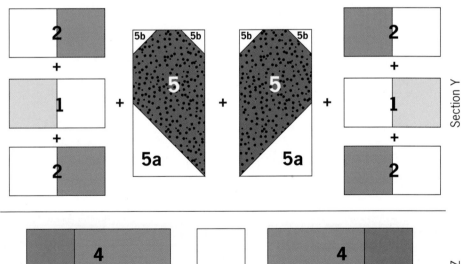
Section Y

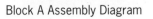

Section Z

Block A Assembly Diagram

Block B Assembly

Assemble this block in sections X, Y, and Z. Section Y is a single piece, Unit 4. Each completed section should measure 14½" wide. Refer to Block B Assembly Diagram throughout.

Sections X and Z

1. For Strip Set 5, join strips of fabrics I and V as shown. Press seam allowances toward Fabric I. Make four of Strip Set 5. From these strip sets, cut sixty-eight 2½"-wide segments for Unit 5.

2. For Section X, join two pair of units 1 and 5 as shown. Sew combined units to opposite sides of one Unit 3.

3. Repeat to make Section Z.

Assembly

Join sections X, Y, and Z to complete block. Make 17 of Block B.

Quilt Assembly

Refer to Row Assembly Diagram for placement of blocks in rows.

1. For Row 1, select three A blocks and two B blocks. Starting with an A block, join blocks as shown, alternating As and Bs. Make four of Row 1.

2. For Row 2, select three B blocks and two A blocks. Starting with a B block, join blocks as shown. Make three of Row 2.

3. Join rows, starting with Row 1 and alternating rows 1 and 2.

Borders

The first two borders are pieced to allow the chain design to continue into the border.

Inner Border

For the first border, make one more strip set. Units from this strip set are pieced with strips 1, 2, and 3 to make inner border. Refer to border diagrams and photo throughout.

1. For Strip Set 6, join strips of fabrics IV and V as shown. Press seam allowances toward Fabric IV. From this, cut ten 2½"-wide segments.

2. To make border for top edge, join one Unit 6 to both ends of one Border 2 strip (Border Diagram 1). Then sew Border 1 strips to both ends of border as shown. Repeat to make bottom border.

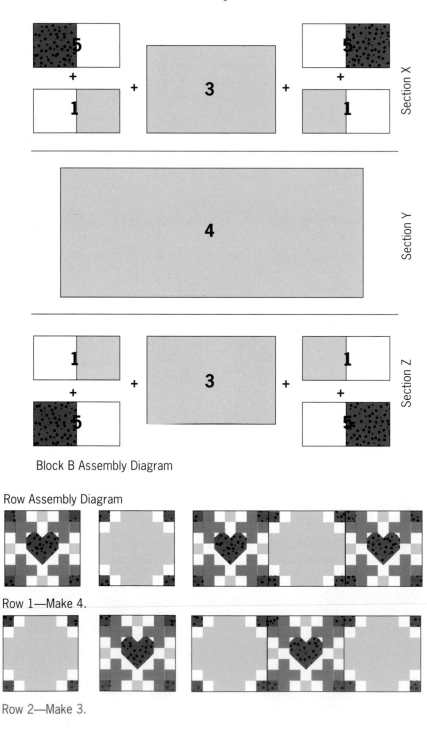

Block B Assembly Diagram

Row Assembly Diagram

Row 1—Make 4.

Row 2—Make 3.

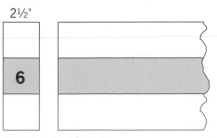

Strip Set 5—Make 4.

Strip Set 6—Make 1.

3. Pin borders to top and bottom edges of quilt, matching Unit 6 seams with seams of Block B. Stitch borders to quilt, easing as needed.

4. To make each side border, join three of Unit 6 and two Border 2 strips as shown (Border Diagram 2). Join a Border 3 strip to both ends to complete each border. Pin borders to quilt sides, matching Unit 6 seams with Block B seams. Stitch borders to quilt, easing as needed.

Middle Border

1. For top border, join one Fabric V square to both ends of a Border 4 strip (Border Diagram 3). Sew Border 4 strips to both ends of border as shown. Repeat for bottom border.

2. Pin borders to top and bottom edges of quilt, matching seams of square with center seams of Unit 6 in first border. Stitch borders to quilt. Trim excess length at ends.

3. For side borders, repeat Step 1. Then add another Fabric V square and one more Border 4 strip to one end of each border.

4. Pin borders to quilt sides, matching seams of square with Unit 6. Stitch borders to quilt sides. Trim excess length at ends.

Outer Border

1. For each side border, join three Fabric III border strips end-to-end. For top and bottom borders, join two strips end-to-end.

2. Referring to instructions on page 17, measure quilt from side to side. Trim top and bottom borders to match width. Sew borders to top and bottom edges of quilt.

3. Measure quilt from top to

bottom. Trim side borders to match length. Sew borders to quilt sides.

Quilting and Finishing

1. Mark quilting design on quilt top as desired. On quilt shown, patchwork and borders are outline-quilted. Use a commercial stencil to mark the heart motif in B blocks.

2. Divide backing into two 3¼-yard lengths. Cut one piece in half lengthwise. Join one narrow panel to each side of wide piece.

3. Layer backing, batting, and quilt top. Baste. Quilt as desired.

4. From reserved strips, make 11 yards of straight-grain binding. See page 22 for instructions on making and applying binding.

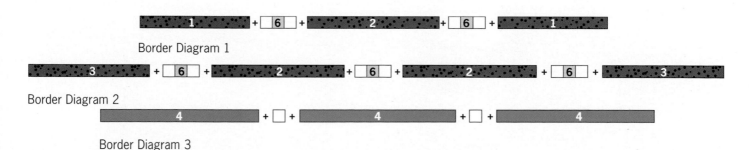

Border Diagram 1

Border Diagram 2

Border Diagram 3

Flying Home

This quilt combines original design with time-honored patchwork. A gaggle of seven quick-pieced birds flies across the top of the quilt, with a single straggler breaking formation. Create the look of filtered sunlight with classic flying geese blocks.

Finished Size

Quilt: 73½" x 109"
Blocks: 8 geese blocks, 15" square
    304 Flying Geese blocks, 2½" x 5"

Materials

	Fabric I (light blue print)	6½ yards
	Fabric II (gray solid)	¼ yard
	Fabric III (black solid)	1¾ yards
	Fabric IV (white-on-white print)	⅛ yard
	Fabric V (brown print)	¾ yard
	Fabric VI (taupe print)	¾ yard
	Fabric VII (rust print)	1⅝ yards
	Fabric VIII (tan print)	⅞ yard
	Fabric IX (gold solid)	¾ yard
	Fabric X (pale yellow print)	¾ yard
	Fabric XI (black/brown print)	⅝ yard
	Backing fabric	6½ yards
	Precut batting	120" x 120"

Quick-Piecing Techniques

Strip Piecing (see page 12)
Diagonal Corners (see page 12)
Diagonal Ends (see page 13)
Triangle-Squares (see page 14)

Cutting

Cut all strips crossgrain, from selvage to selvage. For best use of yardage, cut pieces in order listed. Refer to diagrams to identify pieces.

From Fabric I (light blue print), cut:

✳ Two 15½"-wide strips.
  From one strip, cut:
  • One 15½" x 30½" (Spacer F).
  • Two 5½" x 10½" (Spacer E).
  From second strip, cut:
  • One 15½" square (Spacer H).
  • One 8" x 10½" (Spacer G).
  • One 7½" x 10½" for triangle-squares (A3, A20).
  • Four 7⅛" squares. Cut each square in half diagonally to get eight triangles (A15).

✳ Three 5½"-wide strips. From these, cut:
  • Eight 5½" x 6¾" (A16).
  • One 5½" square (Spacer C).
  • Eight 4¼" x 5½" (A23).
  • Ten 3" x 5½" (A11, Spacer D).

✳ Four 4¼"-wide strips. From these, cut:
  • Eight 4¼" x 10½" (A5).
  • Sixteen 4¼" squares (A4, A22).

✳ Forty-six 3"-wide strips. From these, cut:
  • 616 3" squares (A12c, B1a).
  • Eight 1¾" x 3" (A19).
  • Eight 3" x 4¼" (A9).

✳ Twelve 1¾"-wide strips. Set aside 10 strips for inner border. From two strips, cut:
  • Eight 1¾" x 5½" (A14a).
  • Sixteen 1¾" squares (A1a, A21a).

(continued)

From Fabric II (gray solid), cut:

✳ Two 3"-wide strips. From these, cut:
- Eight 3" x 8½" (A12).
- Four 2⅛" squares. Cut each square in half diagonally to get eight A6 triangles.

From Fabric III (black solid), cut:

✳ One 5½"-wide strip. From this, cut:
- Sixteen 1¾" x 5½" (A1, A21).
- Four 3⅜" squares. Cut each square in half diagonally to get eight triangles (A13).

✳ Sixteen 3"-wide strips. Set aside nine strips for binding. From seven strips, cut:
- Thirty-one 3" x 5½" (B1-1).
- Eight 3" x 3¾" (A12a).
- Eight 3" squares (A9a).
- Eight 1¾" squares (A7).

From Fabric IV (white print), cut:

✳ One 4¼"-wide strip. From this, cut:
- Eight 3" x 4¼" (A12b).
- Four 2⅛" squares. Cut each square in half diagonally to get eight triangles (A8).

From Fabric V (brown print), cut:

✳ One 2¼"-wide strip for Strip Set 1 (A10, A17).

One 7½"-wide strip. From this, cut:
- One 7½" x 10½" for triangle-squares (A3, A20). Use leftover fabric for next cut.

✳ Five 3"-wide strips and two 3" x 30" strips. From these, cut:
- Sixteen 3" x 4¼" (A2, A18).
- Thirty 3" x 5½" (B4-1).

From Fabric VI (taupe print), cut:

✳ One 2½"-wide strip for Strip Set 1 (A10, A17).

✳ Three 5½"-wide strips. From these, cut:
- Thirty-six 3" x 5½" (B5-1).

From Fabric VII (rust print), cut:

✳ Three 5½"-wide strips. From these, cut:
- Twenty-nine 3" x 5½" (B3-1).

✳ Ten 3½"-wide strips for outer border.

From Fabric VIII (tan print), cut:

✳ Four 5½"-wide strips. From these, cut:
- Forty-three 3" x 5½" (B6-1).

✳ Two 1¾"-wide strips. From these, cut:
- Eight 1¾" x 6¾" (A14).

From Fabric IX (gold solid), cut:

✳ Four 5½"-wide strips. From these, cut:
- Forty-four 3" x 5½" (B7-1).

From Fabric X (yellow print), cut:

✳ Four 5½"-wide strips. From these, cut:
- Fifty-one 3" x 5½" (B8-1).

From Fabric XI (brown print), cut:

✳ Three 5½"-wide strips. From these, cut:
- Forty 3" x 5½" (B2-1).

Making Units for Block A

Refer to Block A Assembly Diagram throughout to identify units.

1. On wrong side of 7½" x 10½" piece of Fabric I, draw a 3 x 4-square grid of 2⅛" squares.

2. With right sides facing, match marked piece with corresponding piece of Fabric V. Stitch grid as described on page 14. Cut 24 triangle-squares from grid, three for each block (units A3 and A20). Store triangle-squares in a labelled zip-top bag.

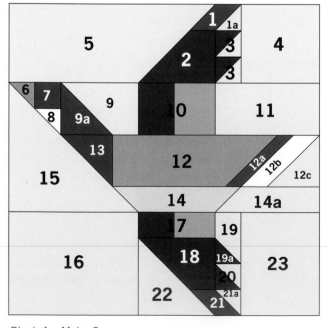

Block A—Make 8.

Block B1—Make 31.

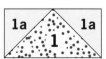

Block B2—Make 40.

Block B3—Make 29.

Block B4—Make 30.

Block B5—Make 36.

Block B6—Make 43.

Block B7—Make 44.

Block B8—Make 51.

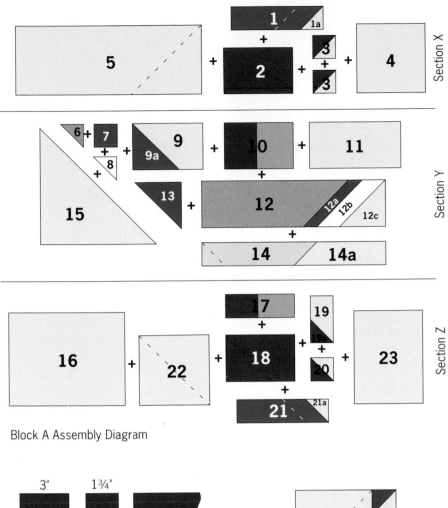

Block A Assembly Diagram

Block A Assembly

Assemble this block in horizontal sections X, Y, and Z. Each completed section should measure approximately 15½" wide. Refer to Block Assembly Diagram throughout.

Section X

1. Join two A3 triangle-squares as shown.

2. Sew Unit 2 to left side of joined squares; press seam allowance toward Unit 2.

3. Join Unit 1 to top of combined unit.

4. Sew Unit 4 to right side of combined unit.

5. Use diagonal-end technique to sew Unit 5 to left side of unit (Unit 5 Diagram). Press; then trim excess fabric from seam allowance.

Section Y

1. Join units 6 and 8 to Square 7.

2. Add Unit 9 to right side of combined unit.

3. Join units 10 and 11 to row as shown.

4. Sew Triangle 13 to Unit 12.

5. Join 12/13 to bottom of first row, aligning right-hand ends of both rows.

6. Add Unit 14 to bottom of combined unit in same manner.

7. Sew Triangle 15 to diagonal edge of combined unit. Press; then trim seam allowance to remove excess fabric from Unit 14.

Section Z

1. Join units 17 and 18 as shown.

2. Sew Unit 20 triangle-square to bottom of Unit 19.

3. Join 19/20 to side of 17/18 as shown. *(continued)*

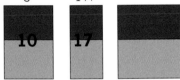

Strip Set 1 Diagram—Make 1.

Unit 5 Diagram

3. Join strips of fabrics V and VI (Strip Set 1 Diagram). From this strip set, cut eight 3"-wide segments (Unit 10) and eight 1¾"-wide segments (Unit 17).

4. Use diagonal-corner technique to make one each of units 1, 9, 19, and 21 as shown.

5. Using diagonal-end technique, make one of Unit 14.

6. Unit 12 combines diagonal-end and diagonal-corner techniques. Use diagonal-end technique to join units 12 and 12a (Unit 12 Diagram). Trim excess fabric from seam allowance and press. Repeat diagonal-end technique to add 12b; trim and press. Use diagonal-corner technique to add 12c as shown.

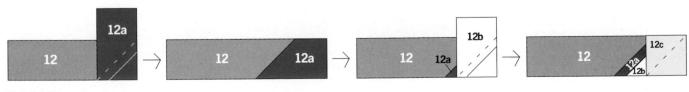

Unit 12 Diagram

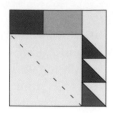

Unit 22 Diagram

4. Join Unit 21 to bottom of combined unit.

5. With right sides facing, align Unit 22 with bottom left corner of combined unit (Unit 22 Diagram). Use diagonal-corner technique to sew Unit 22 as shown. Press. Trim excess fabric from seam allowance.

6. Join units 16 and 23 to sides to complete section.

Assembly

Join sections X, Y, and Z to assemble block. Make eight of Block A.

Block B Assembly

There are eight color variations of Block B. To avoid getting confused, keep each variation in a separate labeled zip-top bag. All variations are sewn in the same manner (Block B Diagrams).

1. For each B1 block, select one Unit 1 of Fabric III and two 1a squares of Fabric I. Use diagonal-corner technique to assemble block as shown. Make 31 of Block B1. For each block, press one seam allowance toward small triangle and the other toward large triangle. (This gives you offset seam allowances when joining blocks. Press all B blocks in same manner.)

2. For B2 block, use one Unit 1 of Fabric XI and two 1a squares of Fabric I. Make 40 of Block B2.

3. For B3 block, use one Unit 1 of Fabric VII and two 1a squares of Fabric I. Make 29 of Block B3.

4. For B4 block, use one Unit 1 of Fabric V and two 1a squares of Fabric I. Make 30 of Block B4.

5. For B5 block, use one Unit 1 of Fabric VI and two 1a squares of Fabric I. Make 36 of Block B5.

6. For B6 block, use one Unit 1 of Fabric VIII and two 1a squares of Fabric I. Make 43 of Block B6.

7. For B7 block, use one Unit 1 of Fabric IX and two 1a squares of Fabric I. Make 44 of Block B7.

8. For B8 block, use one Unit 1 of Fabric X and two 1a squares of Fabric I. Make 51 of Block B8.

Quilt Assembly

Refer to Quilt Assembly Diagram and photo for placement of blocks in rows. Assemble each row from left to right.

Row 1

1. Select four A blocks, three B8 blocks, and one each of spacers C and D.

2. Join B8 blocks and Spacer D in pairs. Join pairs as shown; then sew Spacer C to top of combined units.

3. Add A blocks as shown to complete Row 1.

Row 2

1. From B blocks, select two B6, seven B7, and 11 B8. Then select one each of Block A, Spacer E, and Spacer F.

2. Join three B8 and three B7 blocks in a row as shown.

3. Join two B7 and four B8 blocks in a row.

4. Join both rows of B blocks. Add Spacer E to right side of row.

5. Join two B6, two B7, and four B8 blocks in a row as shown. Add this row to bottom of unit.

6. Join Block A to right side of unit; then add Spacer F to complete Row 2.

Row 3

1. From B blocks, select five B5, eight B6, 11 B7, and 11 B8. Then select one each of Block A and spacers D, G, and H.

2. Join three B6, two B7, three B8, and two more B7 blocks in a row. Add Spacer D to end of row.

3. Join two B5, two B6, three B7, three B8, and one more B7 block in a row.

4. Join both rows. Sew Spacer G to right end of combined row.

5. Join three B5, three B6, three B7, and five B8 in a row. Join this to bottom of combined row.

6. Add Block A and Spacer H as shown to complete Row 3.

Row 4

1. From B blocks, select one B3, four B4, 12 B5, 12 B6, 13 B7, and 14 B8. Then select one each of Block A and Spacer E.

2. Join four B5, three B6, three B7, six B8, and two more B7 blocks in a row.

3. Join two B4, three B5, four B6, four B7, and five B8 blocks in a row.

Block B1—Make 31.

Block B2—Make 40.

Block B3—Make 29.

Block B4—Make 30.

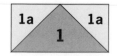
Block B5—Make 36.

Block B6—Make 43.

Block B7—Make 44.

Block B8—Make 51.

4. Join both rows; sew Spacer E to right end of combined row.

5. Join one B3, two B4, five B5, five B6, four B7, and three B8 blocks in a row. Join this to bottom of combined row.

6. Sew Block A to right end of combined row to complete Row 4.

Row 5

1. From B blocks, select three B2, seven B3, eight B4, eight B5, 12 B6, 10 B7, and 12 B8.

2. Join two B3, two B4, and four B5 blocks in a row as shown.

3. Join one B2, two B3, three B4, and two B5 blocks in a row. Join this to bottom of previous row.

4. Join two B2, three B3, and three B4 blocks in a row. Join this to bottom of combined row.

5. Add remaining A block to right side of combined row.

6. Join two B6, two B7, five B8, and three more B7 blocks in a row as shown.

7. Join four B6, three B7, and five B8 blocks in a row. Join this to bottom of previous row.

8. Join two B5, six B6, two B7, and two B8 blocks in a row. Join this to bottom of combined row.

9. Join unit to right side of Block A to complete Row 5.

Rows 6–10 and Assembly

1. For remaining rows, join B blocks as shown in Quilt Assembly Diagram.

2. Join rows as shown.

(continued)

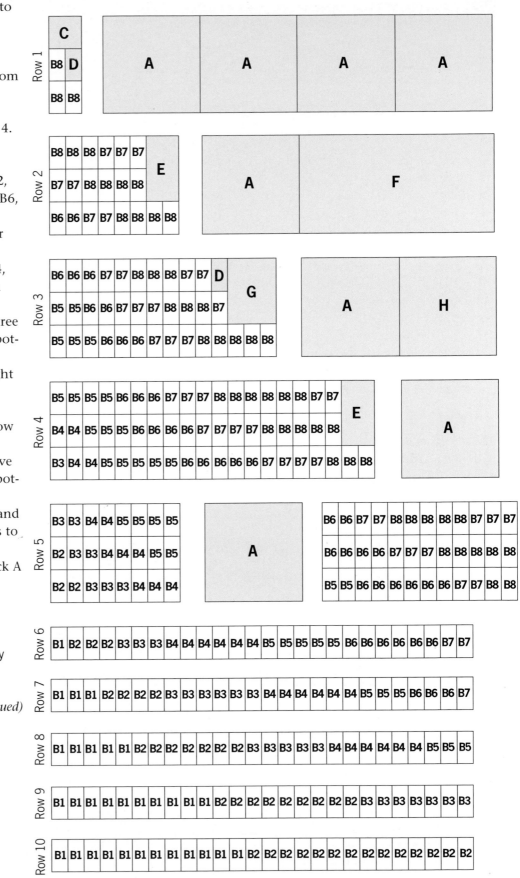

Quilt Assembly Diagram

Borders

1. For inner border, join two 1¾"-wide Fabric I strips end-to-end for top and bottom borders. Join three strips for each side border.

2. Referring to instructions on page 17, measure quilt from side to side. Measuring outward from center seam, trim top and bottom borders to match width. Matching centers, sew borders to top and bottom edges of quilt.

3. Measure quilt from top to bottom; then trim remaining borders to match quilt length. Sew borders to quilt sides. Press seam allowances toward borders.

4. For outer border, piece 3½"-wide strips of Fabric VII in same manner as for inner border. Trim borders to fit. Sew to quilt in same manner.

Quilting and Finishing

1. Mark quilting design on quilt top as desired. Quilt shown is outline-quilted, with two geese outlines quilted in Spacer F. Wavy lines of air currents are quilted around each goose.

2. Divide backing into two 3¼-yard lengths. Cut one piece in half lengthwise. Join one narrow panel to each side of wide piece to assemble backing.

3. Layer backing, batting, and quilt top. Baste. Quilt as marked or as desired.

4. From reserved strips, make 11 yards of binding. See page 22 for instructions on making and applying straight-grain binding.

Baby Buggies Crib Set

Personalize each pretty pram in this crib quilt with bits of ribbon and lace. Coordinating bumper pads (instructions included) make this sweet set ready for dreamland.

Finished Size
Quilt: 48" x 50"
Blocks: 6 buggy blocks, 12" x 14"

Materials

	Fabric I (peach solid)	1¼ yards
	Fabric II (dark peach solid)	1½ yards
	Fabric III (mint green solid)	¼ yard
	Fabric IV (green print for one buggy, border)	½ yard
	Fabric V (two peach prints)	¼ yard each
	Fabric VI (three assorted green prints)	¼ yard each
	Fabric VII (muslin)	¼ yard
	Fabric VIII (mint green print)	⅜ yard
	Backing fabric	3 yards
	1½"-wide beaded lace trim	1½ yards
	⅝"-wide mint green satin ribbon	½ yard
	⅝"-wide peach satin ribbon	1 yard
	Precut batting	72" x 90"

Quick-Piecing Techniques
Diagonal Corners (see page 12)
Triangle-Squares (see page 14)

Cutting
Cut all strips crossgrain, from selvage to selvage, except as noted. For best use of yardage, cut pieces in order listed. Refer to block and quilt assembly diagrams to identify pieces.

From Fabric I (peach solid), cut:
✴ One 5½"-wide strip. From this, cut:
  • Six 5½" x 6½" (A3, B3).
✴ Ten 2½"-wide strips. Set aside five strips for inner border and horizontal sashing. From remaining strips, cut:
  • Four 2½" x 14½" (sashing).
  • Eighteen 2½" x 3½" (A11, B11).
  • Eighteen 2½" squares (A1a, A4a, B1a, B4a).
✴ Four 1½"-wide strips. From these, cut:
  • Six 1½" x 4½" (A7, B7).
  • Twelve 1½" x 3½" (A5, B5).
  • Forty-eight 1½" squares (A8a, B8a).

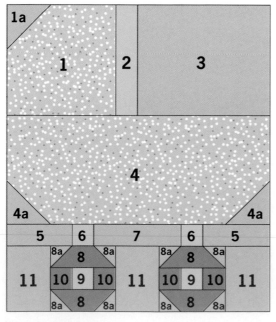

Block A—Make 2.

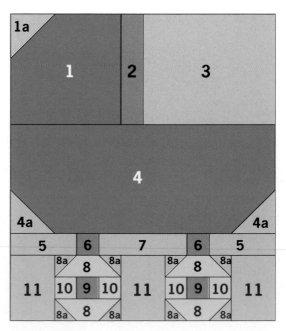

Block B—Make 4.

From Fabric II (dark peach solid), cut:

* Four 2" x 52" lengthwise strips for outer border.
* Four 3" x 52" lengthwise strips for straight-grain binding.
* One 7" x 27" lengthwise strip for triangle-squares.
* Seven 1½" x 15" strips. From these, cut:
  * Four 1½" x 5½" (B2).
  * Eight 1½" x 3½" (A8).
  * Twenty-four 1½" squares (A10, B6, B9).

From Fabric III (green solid), cut:

* Three 1½"-wide strips. From these, cut:
  * Two 1½" x 5½" (A2).
  * Sixteen 1½" x 3½" (B8).
  * Twenty-four 1½" squares (A6, A9, B10).

From Fabric IV (green print), cut:

* One 12½" square. From this, cut:
  * One 5½" x 12½" (B4).
  * One 5½" square (B1).
* Eight 2" x 26" strips for middle border.

From Fabric V (peach prints), cut:

* Two 5½" x 12½" (A4).
* Two 5½" squares (A1).

From Fabric VI (green prints), cut:

* Three 5½" x 12½" (B4).
* Three 5½" squares (B1).

From Fabric VII (muslin), cut:

* One 7" x 27" strip for triangle-squares.

From Fabric VIII (mint green), cut:

* Ten 4½" squares (pieced sashing).

Units for Block A

Refer to Block A Assembly Diagram throughout to identify units.

1. Use diagonal-corner technique to make one each of units 1 and 4 as shown.

2. Use diagonal-corner technique to make four of Unit 8.

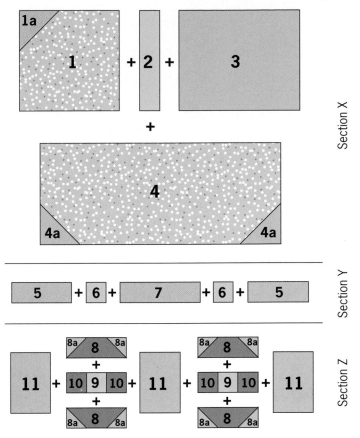

Block A Assembly Diagram

Block A Assembly

Assemble this block in horizontal sections X, Y, and Z. Each completed section should measure 12½" wide. Refer to Block A Assembly Diagram throughout.

Section X

1. Join Unit 1 to one side of Unit 2.

2. Sew Unit 3 to opposite side of Unit 2 as shown. Press seam allowances away from Unit 2.

3. Join Unit 4 to bottom of combined unit. Press seam allowance toward Unit 4.

Section Y

1. Join one of Unit 6 to both ends of Unit 7.

2. Add one Unit 5 to both ends of row.

3. Press seam allowances away from Unit 6.

Section Z

1. Join one of Unit 10 to both sides of Unit 9 as shown. Make two 9/10 units, one for each wheel.

2. Sew one of Unit 8 to top edges of both 9/10 units. Repeat for bottom edges. Press seam allowances away from Unit 8.

3. Join combined units with three of Unit 11 in a row as shown.

Assembly

Join sections to assemble block. Make two of Block A.

Block B Assembly

Refer to Block B Diagram to identify units.

1. Use diagonal-corner technique to make one each of units 1 and 4 as shown.

2. Use diagonal-corner technique to make four of Unit 8.

3. Assemble Block B in same manner as for Block A. Make four of Block B.

(continued)

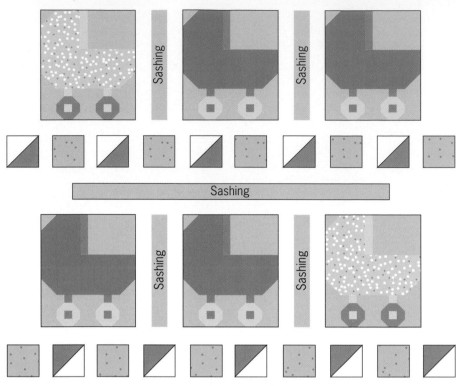

Quilt Assembly Diagram

Quilt Assembly

Refer to Quilt Assembly Diagram for placement of blocks in rows. Assemble each row from left to right.

1. For top row, select one A block, two B blocks, and two 14½"-long sashing strips. Join blocks and sashing strips in a row as shown. In same manner, join remaining blocks and sashing strips for second row. Press seam allowances toward sashing.

2. On wrong side of 7" x 27" piece of muslin, draw a 1 x 5-square grid of 4⅞" squares. With right sides facing, match marked piece with corresponding piece of Fabric II. Stitch grid as described on page 14. Cut 10 triangle-squares from grid, five for each row of pieced sashing.

3. For top row of pieced sashing, select five triangle-squares and five squares of Fabric VIII. Starting with a triangle-square, join squares in a row, alternating triangle-squares and plain squares as shown.

4. For bottom row of pieced sashing, join remaining squares and triangle-squares as shown.

5. Join rows from top to bottom as shown, adding horizontal strip of sashing in center as shown.

Borders

1. Referring to instructions on page 17, measure quilt from side to side. Trim two 2½"-wide Fabric I strips to match width. Sew borders to top and bottom edges of quilt.

2. Measure quilt from top to bottom; then trim remaining borders to match quilt length. Sew borders to quilt sides. Press seam allowances toward borders.

3. For middle border, piece two Fabric IV strips end-to-end to make one strip for each side of quilt. Measure quilt as before; then trim borders to fit and sew to quilt in same manner.

4. For outer border, measure quilt and trim Fabric II strips to fit. Sew borders to quilt as before.

Quilting and Finishing

1. Mark quilting design on quilt top as desired. Quilt shown is outline-quilted.

2. Divide backing into two 1½-yard lengths. Cut one panel in half lengthwise, discarding one half. Join remaining half panel to full piece to assemble backing with an off-center seam.

3. Layer backing, batting, and quilt top. Baste. Quilt as marked or as desired.

4. From reserved strips, make 5¾ yards of binding. See page 22 for instructions on making and applying straight-grain binding.

5. Cut lace trim into 9" lengths. Turn under 1" at ends of each piece. Tack one piece of trim to edge of each Unit 2 as shown.

6. Cut ribbons into 9" lengths. Tie each piece into a bow. Tack one bow center to bottom of each Unit 2 as shown.

Crib Bumpers

These instructions are for two 8" x 28" bumpers and two 8" x 52" bumpers. Adjust yardage and instructions as necessary to make different sizes.

To make bumpers that coordinate with the crib quilt, you'll need the following:

✱ ¾ yard each of fabrics I, II, and VIII for patchwork.

✱ 1½ yards of Fabric III for backing and ties.

✱ ¾ yard of muslin and ⅝ yard of 60"-wide low-loft batting for quilting.

✱ 1⅛ yards of 60"-wide high-loft batting for padding.

1. From Fabric I, cut two 12" x 27" strips for triangle-squares. Cut matching pieces from Fabric II.

2. On wrong side of one Fabric I piece, draw a 2 x 5-square grid of

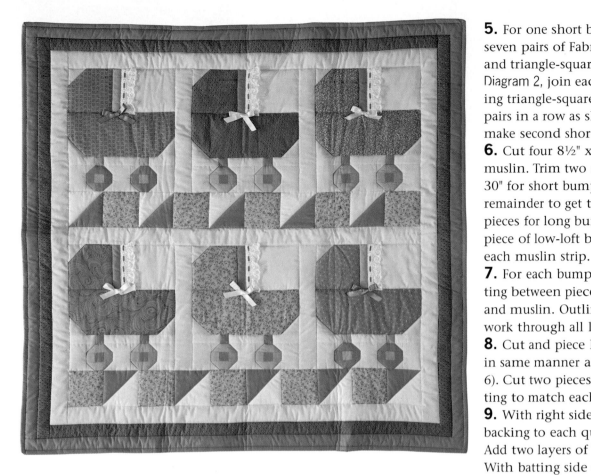

5. For one short bumper pad, select seven pairs of Fabric VIII squares and triangle-squares. Referring to Diagram 2, join each pair, positioning triangle-squares as shown. Join pairs in a row as shown. Repeat to make second short bumper.

6. Cut four 8½" x 42" strips of muslin. Trim two strips to 8½" x 30" for short bumpers. Piece remainder to get two 8½" x 54" pieces for long bumpers. Cut one piece of low-loft batting to match each muslin strip.

7. For each bumper, sandwich batting between pieced front (faceup) and muslin. Outline-quilt patchwork through all layers.

8. Cut and piece Fabric III backing in same manner as for muslin (Step 6). Cut two pieces of high-loft batting to match each backing strip.

9. With right sides facing, match backing to each quilted bumper. Add two layers of batting and pin. With batting side down, stitch around bumper through all layers, leaving a 7"-wide opening on one long side. Clip corners and turn right side out. Press lightly. Slipstitch openings closed.

10. For ties, cut sixteen 1½" x 21" strips from remaining Fabric III. Press under ¼" on all edges of each strip.

11. With wrong sides facing, press each strip in half lengthwise. Topstitch all pressed edges. Pin center of one tie to back of each bumper corner and topstitch to secure.

4⅞" squares. With right sides facing, match marked piece with Fabric II piece. Sew grid as shown on page 14. Cut 20 triangle-squares from grid. Use remaining pieces to stitch a second grid to get a total of 40 triangle-squares.

3. From Fabric VIII, cut forty 4½" squares.

4. For one long bumper pad, select 13 pairs of Fabric VIII squares and triangle-squares. Referring to Diagram 1, join each pair, taking care to position triangle-squares as shown. Join pairs in a row as shown. Repeat to make second long bumper.

Diagram 1

Diagram 2

Flowers
in the Cabin

The time-honored Log Cabin block is new again. Use different-width strips to create an illusion of circles without sewing any curves at all. Sashing gives the quilt an open and airy look.

Finished Size

Quilt: 75" x 107"
Blocks: 96 Log Cabin blocks, 7½" square
　　　　4 corner blocks, 4" square

Quick-Piecing Technique

Strip Piecing (see page 12)

Materials

Fabric I (muslin or white-on-white)	5⅛ yards	
Fabric II (slate blue solid)	2¾ yards	
Fabric III (blue-on-ivory print)	3⅛ yards	
Fabric IV (light blue solid)	¼ yard	
Fabric V (gold print)	¾ yard	
Backing fabric	6½ yards	
Precut batting	90" x 108"	

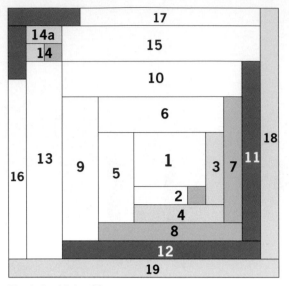

Block A—Make 60.

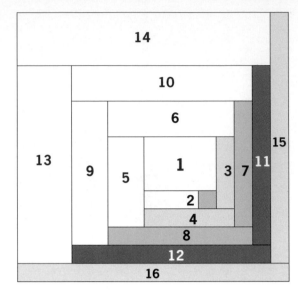

Block B—Make 36.

Cutting

Cut all strips crossgrain, from selvage to selvage. For best use of yardage, cut pieces in order listed. Refer to block diagrams to identify pieces.

From Fabric I (muslin), cut:

✳ Four 5½"-wide strips for strip sets 3 and 4.
✳ Twenty-two 2"-wide strips. Set aside three strips for Strip Set 1. From remaining strips, cut:
  • Thirty-six 2" x 7½" (B14).
  • Thirty-six 2" x 6" (B13).
  • Ninety-six 2" x 2½" (A1, B1).
✳ Seventy-two 1½"-wide strips. From these, cut:
  • Thirty-eight 1½" x 15½" for sashing.
  • 120 1½" x 6" (A13, A15).
  • Ninety-six 1½" x 5½" (A10, B10).
  • Ninety-six 1½" x 4½" (A9, B9).
  • Ninety-six 1½" x 4" (A6, B6).
  • Ninety-six 1½" x 3" (A5, B5).
  • Four 1" x 1½" (C3).
  • Four 1" squares (C2).

From Fabric II (slate blue), cut:

✳ Nine 3"-wide strips for binding.
✳ Two 2½"-wide strips for Strip Set 4.
✳ Two 2"-wide strips for Strip Set 3.
✳ Twenty 1½"-wide strips for borders.
✳ Twenty-eight 1"-wide strips. From these, cut:
  • Ninety-six 1" x 6" (A12, B12).
  • Ninety-six 1" x 5½" (A11, B11).
  • Four 1" x 2½" (C7).
  • Four 1" x 2" (C6).

From Fabric III (ivory print), cut:

✳ Ten 4½"-wide strips for middle border.
✳ One 2"-wide strip. From this, cut:
  • Four 2" x 4½" (C11).
  • Four 2" x 3" (C10).
✳ Fifty-four 1"-wide strips. Set aside two strips for Strip Set 2. From remaining strips, cut:
  • Ninety-six 1" x 8" (A19, B16).
  • Ninety-six 1" x 7½" (A18, B15).
  • 100 1" x 3" (A4, B4, C9).
  • 100 1" x 2½" (A3, B3, C8).
  • Four 1" x 2" (C5).
  • Sixty-four 1" x 1½" (A14a, C4).

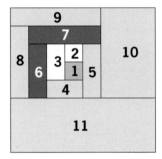

Block C—Make 4.

From Fabric IV (light blue), cut:

✳ Five 1"-wide strips for strip sets 1 and 2. From ends of these strips, cut:
  • Four 1" squares (C1).

From Fabric V (gold print), cut:

✳ One 1½"-wide strip. From this, cut:
  • Fifteen 1½" squares for sashing.
✳ Twenty-one 1" x 42" strips. From these, cut:
  • Ninety-six 1" x 4½" (A8, B8).
  • Ninety-six 1" x 4" (A7, B7).

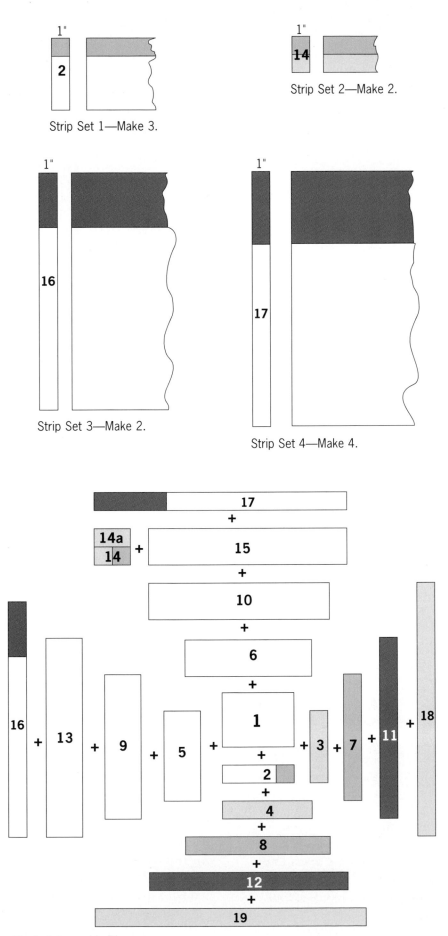

1"
2

Strip Set 1—Make 3.

1"
14

Strip Set 2—Make 2.

1"
16

Strip Set 3—Make 2.

1"
17

Strip Set 4—Make 4.

17

+

| 14a / 14 | + | 15 |

+

| 10 |

+

| 6 |

+

| 16 | + | 13 | + | 9 | + | 5 | + | 1 | + | 3 | + | 7 | + | 11 | + | 18 |

| 2 |

+

| 4 |

+

| 8 |

+

| 12 |

+

| 19 |

Block A Assembly Diagram

Strip Sets

Refer to strip set diagrams and Block A Assembly Diagram throughout to identify units. Store units cut from each strip set in zip-top bags.

1. For Strip Set 1, join strips of fabrics I and IV as shown. Make three of Strip Set 1. Press seam allowances toward Fabric IV. From these strip sets, cut ninety-six 1"-wide segments for Unit 2.

2. For Strip Set 2, join strips of fabrics III and IV as shown. Make two of Strip Set 2. Press seam allowances toward Fabric III. From these strip sets, cut sixty 1"-wide segments for Unit 14.

3. For Strip Set 3, join 5½"-wide strip of Fabric I and 2"-wide strip of Fabric II as shown. Make two of Strip Set 3. Press seam allowances toward Fabric II. From these strip sets, cut sixty 1"-wide segments for Unit 16.

4. For Strip Set 4, join 5½"-wide strip of Fabric I and 2½"-wide strip of Fabric II as shown. Make two of Strip Set 4. From these, cut sixty 1"-wide segments for Unit 17.

Block A Assembly

Assemble this block from the center out. Each completed block should measure approximately 8" square. Refer to Block A Assembly Diagram throughout.

1. Join units in numerical order as shown. Work around the block up to Unit 13. As strips are added, press seam allowances toward the strip just added.

2. Join Unit 14 to 14a. Press seam allowance toward 14a. Join combined Unit 14 to one end of Unit 15, and press seam allowance toward Unit 15. Stitch 14/15 to block as shown.

3. Add units 16–19 as shown to complete block.

4. Make 60 of Block A.

(continued)

Block B Assembly

Assemble this block like Block A, but without the corner "flower." Each completed block should measure 8" square.

Referring to Block B Assembly Diagram, join units in numerical order as shown. Press seam allowances toward each new strip. Make 36 of Block B.

Block C Assembly

Positioned in the border corners, this block is a smaller version of Block A. Each completed block should measure approximately 4½" square. Referring to Block C Assembly Diagram, join units in numerical order as shown. Make four of Block C.

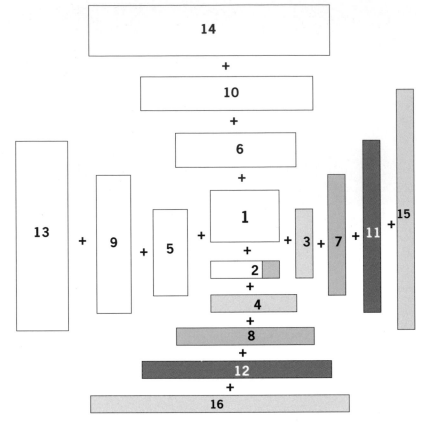

Block B Assembly Diagram

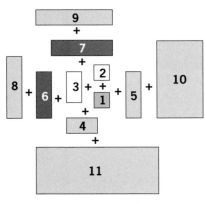

Block C Assembly Diagram

Quilt Assembly

Refer to Row Assembly Diagram for placement of blocks in rows. Be careful to turn each block as shown for correct position. Assemble each row from left to right.

1. For Row 1, select six A blocks, 10 B blocks, and three Fabric I sashing strips. Join blocks in groups of four as shown, making four 15½" squares. Join squares in a row with sashing between squares as shown. Press seam allowances toward sashing strips. Make two of Row 1.

2. For Row 2, select 12 A blocks, four B blocks, and three sashing strips. Join blocks in groups of four as shown. Join squares in a row

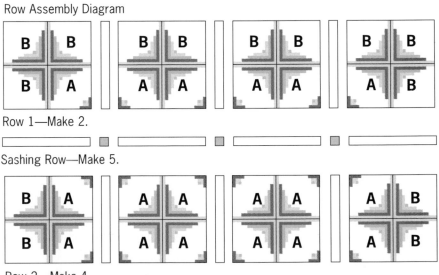

Row Assembly Diagram

Row 1—Make 2.

Sashing Row—Make 5.

Row 2—Make 4.

with sashing strips between squares. Make four of Row 2.

3. For Sashing Row, select four sashing strips and three Fabric V sashing squares. Join strips and squares in a row as shown. Press seam allowances toward sashing strips. Make five Sashing Rows.

4. Referring to photo, lay out four of Row 2. Position one of Row 1 at top and bottom. Place a Sashing Row between all rows. When satisfied with row placement, join rows.

Borders

1. For inner border, join three 1½"-wide strips of Fabric II end-to-end for each side border. Join two strips for top and bottom borders.

2. Referring to instructions on page 17, measure quilt from top to bottom. Measuring outward from center of border strips, trim side borders to match length. Matching centers, sew borders to quilt sides.

3. Measure quilt from side to side; then trim remaining borders to match quilt width. Sew borders to top and bottom edges. Press seam allowances toward border.

4. For middle border, repeat Step 1 with 4½"-wide strips of Fabric III.

Measure quilt from top to bottom and trim longer strips to match length. Measure quilt from side to side and trim shorter borders to match width.

5. Stitch shorter borders to top and bottom edges of quilt.

6. Referring to photo, join Block C to ends of each side border. Then sew borders to quilt sides.

7. For outer border, repeat steps 1 and 2.

Quilting and Finishing

1. Mark quilting design on quilt top as desired. On quilt shown, patchwork is outline-quilted and three concentric circles are quilted around each flower. Centered on the sashing squares, circles are 5¾", 9¾", and 13¾" in diameter. Look for plates, bowls, pots, or other objects that can be ready-made templates for marking circles.

2. Divide backing into two 3¼-yard lengths. Cut one piece in half lengthwise. Join one narrow panel to each side of wide piece.

3. Layer backing, batting, and quilt top. Baste. Quilt as marked or as desired.

4. From Fabric II strips, make 10½ yards of straight-grain binding. See page 22 for instructions on making and applying binding.

Pinwheels

This updated version of the traditional Drunkard's Path has no curved seams. Quick-piecing eliminates the difficulty of cutting and sewing curves. Choose two shades of your favorite color to make your own all-new classic quilt.

Finished Size
Quilt: 81" x 99"
Blocks: 36 pinwheel blocks, 9" square

Materials

■	Fabric I (burgundy print)	5⅛ yards
▨	Fabric II (rose print)	3⅛ yards
□	Fabric III (white-on-white print)	2⅜ yards
	Backing fabric	6 yards
	Precut batting	90" x 108"

Cutting
Cut all strips crossgrain, from selvage to selvage, except as noted. For best use of yardage, cut pieces in order listed. Refer to block diagrams to identify pieces.

Green

From Fabric I (burgundy print), cut:
✳ Two 9½" x 83" lengthwise strips and two 9½" x 65" lengthwise strips for border.
✳ Four 2¾"-wide strips. From these and fabric left over from border, cut:
  • 124 2¾" squares (B1a).

Brown

From Fabric II (rose print), cut:
✳ Eight 9½" x 42" strips. From these, cut:
  • Thirty-one 9½" squares (B1).
✳ Fourteen 2"-wide strips. From these, cut:
  • 288 2" squares (A4).

✳ Forty-two 1¼"-wide strips. From these, cut:
  • 288 1¼" x 2¾" pieces (A3).
  • 288 1¼" x 2" pieces (A2).
  • 288 1¼" squares (A1a).
✳ Nine 3"-wide strips for binding.

Quick-Piecing Techniques
Diagonal Corners (see page 12)

From Fabric III (white-on-white print), cut:
✳ Thirty-two 2"-wide strips. From these, cut:
  • 144 2" x 2¾" pieces (A6).
  • 288 2" squares (A1).
  • 288 1¼" x 2" pieces (A5).
✳ Nine 1¼"-wide strips. From these, cut:
  • 288 1¼" squares (A4a).

(continued)

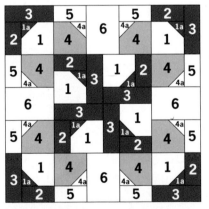

Block A—Make 36.

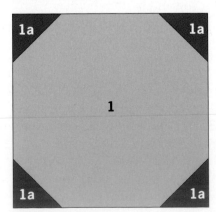

Block B—Make 31.

Units for Block A

Refer to Block A Assembly Diagram throughout to identify units.

1. Use diagonal-corner technique to make eight of Unit 1.

2. Use diagonal-corner technique to make eight of Unit 4.

Block A Assembly

Assemble this block in sections X, Y, and Z. Each completed section should measure approximately 9½" wide. Refer to Block A Assembly Diagram throughout.

Sections X and Z

Assemble Section X from left to right. Make Section Z with the same units in the same manner.

1. Join units 1 and 2. Press seam allowance toward Unit 2.

2. Add Unit 3 to top of combined unit as shown. Press seam allowances toward Unit 3.

3. Make a second 1/2/3 unit in same manner.

4. Join Unit 5 to top of Unit 4 as shown. Make a second 4/5 unit. Press seam allowances toward Unit 5.

5. To complete Section X, join combined units in a row as shown, with Unit 6 in middle of row. Press joining seam allowances away from 4/5 units.

6. Repeat steps 1–5 above to assemble Section Z.

Section Y

Assemble the center of the section first; then the outer rows.

1. Follow steps 1 and 2 above to make four 1/2/3 units.

2. Join four units as shown. Press joining seams toward Unit 3s.

3. Join a Unit 5 to one Unit 4. Make four 4/5 units.

4. Sew a 4/5 unit to opposite sides of Unit 6. Make two 4/5/6 units.

5. Join 4/5/6 units to opposite sides of center as shown to complete section.

Assembly

Join sections X, Y, and Z to complete block. Make 36 of Block A.

Block B Assembly

Use diagonal-corner technique to make one block as shown. Make 31 of Block B.

Quilt Assembly

Refer to Row Assembly Diagram for placement of blocks in rows. Assemble each row from left to right.

1. Set aside four A blocks for border.

2. For Row 1, select four A blocks and three B blocks. Starting with an A block, join blocks as shown, alternating As and Bs. Make five of Row 1.

3. For Row 2, select three of Block A and four of Block B. Starting with a B block, join blocks as shown, alternating Bs and As. Make four of Row 2.

4. Join rows, starting with Row 1 and alternating rows 1 and 2.

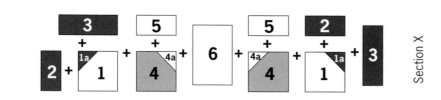

Section X

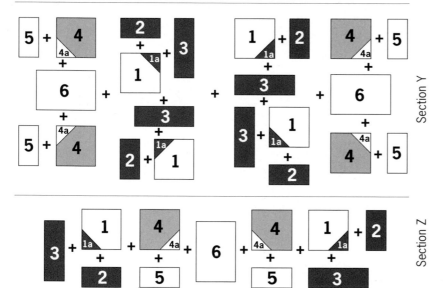

Section Y

Section Z

Block A Assembly Diagram

Row Assembly Diagram

Row 1—Make 5.

Row 2—Make 4.

Borders

1. Referring to instructions on page 17, measure quilt from top to bottom. Trim 83"-long border strips to match length.

2. Measure quilt from side to side. Trim 65"-long borders to match quilt width.

3. Sew longer borders to quilt sides. Press seam allowances toward borders.

4. Join A blocks to both ends of each remaining border. Press seam allowances away from blocks.

5. Sew pieced borders to top and bottom edges of quilt.

Quilting and Finishing

1. Mark quilting design on quilt top as desired. On quilt shown, patchwork is outline-quilted and a wave pattern is quilted in borders.

2. Divide backing into two 3-yard lengths. Cut one piece in half lengthwise. Join one narrow panel to each side of wide piece to assemble backing.

3. Layer backing, batting, and quilt top. Baste. Quilt as marked or as desired.

4. From Fabric I strips, make 10¼ yards of straight-grain binding. See page 22 for instructions on making and applying binding.

Counting Sheep

*Sweet dreams come to one who sleeps with these
little lambs. Use three quick-piecing methods to make the flock and flowers,
and you'll be counting sheep in no time.*

Finished Size
Quilt: 68¼" x 105"
Blocks: 6 white sheep blocks, 13½" x 15"
      7 black sheep blocks, 9¾" x 13½"
      38 flower blocks, 5¼" x 6"

Materials

Fabric I (black solid)	2½ yards
Fabric II (white-on-white)	1¼ yards
Fabric III (light green solid)	2¼ yards
Fabric IV (gray print)	⅜ yard
Fabric V (yellow print)	3 yards
Fabric VI (gold print)	½ yard
Fabric VII (olive print)	⅝ yard
Fabric VIII (dark green print)	¾ yard
Backing fabric	6½ yards
Precut batting	90" x 108"

Quick-Piecing Techniques
Strip Piecing (see page 12)
Diagonal Corners (see page 12)
Diagonal Ends (see page 13)

Cutting
Cut all strips crossgrain, from selvage to selvage. For best use of yardage, cut pieces in order listed. Refer to diagrams to identify pieces.

From Fabric I (black), cut:
* Thirteen 3½"-wide strips. Set aside 10 strips for borders. From remaining strips, cut:
  * Seven 3½" x 5¾" (C7).
  * Twenty-eight 2¾" x 3½" (C12).
* One 2¾"-wide strip. From this, cut:
  * Fourteen 2¾" squares (C13).
* Two 2"-wide strips. From these, cut:
  * Six 2" x 3½" (A1, B1).
  * Twelve 2" x 2½" (A12, B12).
  * Twenty 1¼" x 2" (A4, B4, C4a).
* Six 1¼"-wide strips. From these, cut:
  * Fourteen 1¼" x 3½" (C3).
  * Thirteen 1¼" x 2¾" (A14a, B14a, C9).
  * 110 1¼" squares (A5a, B5a, A6b, B6b, A7a, B7a, A8a, B8a, C2b, C5a, C8a).
* Nine 3"-wide strips for binding.

(continued)

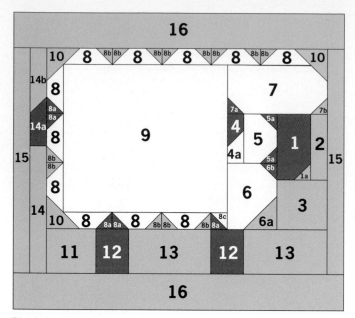

Block A—Make 3.

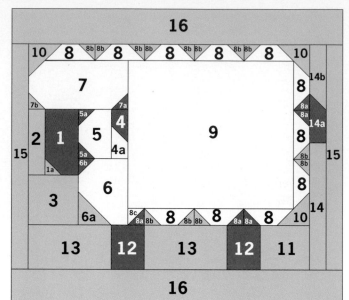

Block B—Make 3.

From Fabric II (white), cut:

❋ One 8"-wide strip. From this, cut:
- Six 7¼" x 8" (A9, B9).

❋ Five 2¾"-wide strips. From these, cut:
- Six 2¾" x 5" (A7, B7).
- Seven 2¾" x 4¼" (C6).
- Six 2¾" x 3½" (A6, B6).
- Twenty 2" x 2¾" (A5, B5, C2).
- Sixty-six 1¼" x 2¾" (A8, B8).
- Six 1¼" x 2" (A4a, B4a).

❋ Four ⅞"-wide strips for Strip Set 1.

❋ Twelve 1⅝"-wide strips. From these, cut:
- 152 1⅝" x 2" (D5).
- 152 1¼" x 1⅝" (D2a).
- Six 1¼" squares (A8c, B8c).

From Fabric III (light green), cut:

❋ One 11¾"-wide strip. From this, cut:
- Two 11¾" x 14" (Spacer E).
- Six 1¼" x 14" (Spacer F).

❋ Three 3⅛"-wide strips. From these, cut:
- Eight 3⅛" x 14" (Spacer G).

❋ Three 2¾"-wide strips. From these, cut:
- Twenty-seven 2¾" squares (A3, B3, C10).
- Fourteen 2" x 2¾" (C11).

❋ Six 2⅛"-wide strips. From these, cut:
- Twelve 2⅛" x 15½" (A16, B16).

❋ Two 2½"-wide strips. From these, cut:
- Twelve 2½" x 4¼" (A13, B13).
- Six 2½" x 2¾" (A11, B11).

❋ Three 1¾"-wide strips. From these, cut:
- Twelve 1¾" x 10¾" (A15, B15).

❋ Twelve 1¼"-wide strips. From these, cut:
- Fourteen 1¼" x 10¼" (C14).
- Six 1¼" x 6¼" (A14, B14).
- Twelve 1¼" x 3½" (A2, A14b, B2, B14b).
- Fourteen 1¼" x 2" (C1).
- 174 1¼" squares (A1a, A7b, A8b, B1a, B7b, B8b, C2a, C6a, C12b, C13a).

❋ From scraps, cut:
- Fifty-two 2" squares (A6a, B6a, A10, B10, C12a).

From Fabric IV (gray print), cut:

❋ One 3½"-wide strip. From this, cut:
- Fourteen 2" x 3½" (C8).
- Two 1¼" x 10" strips. From these, cut fourteen 1¼" squares (C6b).

❋ One 2¾" strip. From this, cut:
- Seven 2¾" squares (C5).
- Fourteen 1¼" x 2¾" (C4).

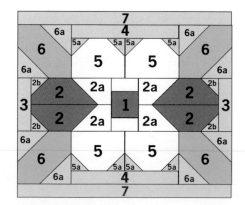

Block C—Make 7.

Block D—Make 38.

From Fabric V (yellow print), cut:

✶ Nine 5¾"-wide strips. From these, cut:
- Twenty-four 5" x 5¾" (Sashing 3).
- Forty 4¼" x 5¾" (Sashing 2).
- Twelve 3⅛" x 5¾" (Sashing 1).

✶ Two 6½"-wide strips. From these, cut:
- Seventy-six ⅞" x 6½" (D7).

✶ Ten 1⅜" strips. From these and scraps, cut:
- 304 1⅜" squares (D6a).

✶ Eleven 1"-wide strips. From these, cut:
- 456 1" squares (D2b, D5a).

✶ Ten ⅞"-wide strips. From these, cut:
- Seventy-six ⅞" x 3½" (D4).
- Seventy-six ⅞" x 2" (D3).

From Fabric VI (gold print), cut:

✶ Two 1¼"-wide strips for Strip Set 1.

✶ Nine 1¼"-wide strips. From these, cut:
- 152 1¼" x 2⅜" (D2).

From Fabric VII (olive print), cut:

✶ Eight 2"-wide strips. From these, cut:
- 152 2" squares (D6).

From Fabric VIII (dark green), cut:

✶ Four 5¾"-wide strips. From these, cut:
- Twenty-four 5¾" squares for sashing.

Units for Block A

Refer to Block A Assembly Diagram throughout to identify units.

1. Use diagonal-corner technique to make one each of units 1, 5, 6, and 7. Be sure to place appropriate fabric in each corner as shown.

2. Use diagonal-corner technique to make 11 of Unit 8. Make two units with one 8a corner, three units with one 8b corner, four units with two 8b corners, and two units with one each of 8a and 8b corners (see diagram for fabric placement).

3. Place one 8a and one 8c together with right sides facing. Stitch a diagonal seam through center, like a diagonal corner. Trim excess fabric from seam allowance and press to get a triangle-square as shown.

4. Use diagonal-end technique to make one each of units 4 and 14.

Block A Assembly

Refer to Block A Assembly Diagram throughout to identify units. Each completed block should measure approximately 14" x 15½".

1. Join units 1 and 2. Add Unit 3 to bottom of 1/2 unit.

2. Join units 4 and 5. Add Unit 6 to bottom of 4/5 unit.

3. Join combined unit 1/2/3 to right side of unit 4/5/6.

4. Join Unit 7 to top of combined unit to complete head section.

5. For bottom of Unit 9, select three of Unit 8—one with one 8a corner, one with two 8b corners, and one with 8a/8b corners. Referring to diagram, join three units in a horizontal row. Join Unit 8a/8c to right end as shown. Sew row to bottom of Unit 9.

6. For side of Unit 9, select three of Unit 8—one with one 8a corner, one with one 8b corner, and one with 8a/8b corners. Join units in a vertical row as shown. Sew row to left side of Unit 9.

7. Join 8/9 unit to head section.

8. Join five remaining Unit 8s in a horizontal row. Sew row to top of combined body section.

9. Sew Unit 10 to three corners of body section as shown.

10. Join units 11, 12, and 13 in a row as shown. Sew row to bottom of body section.

11. Sew units 14 and 15 to left side of body section. Sew Unit 15 to right side.

12. Sew Unit 16s to top and bottom edges to complete block.

13. Make three of Block A.

(continued)

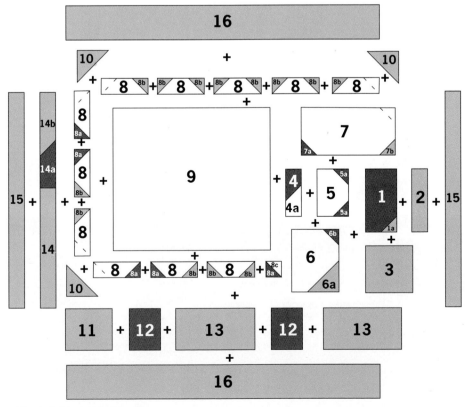

Block A Assembly Diagram

Block B Assembly

Block B is a mirror image of Block A. Make most units exactly the same as for Block A, but reverse angles of diagonal corners and diagonal ends. Refer to Block B Diagram carefully when making units 1, 4, 6, 7, 8, and 14. Make three of Block B.

Units for Block C

Refer to Block C Assembly Diagram throughout to identify units.

1. Use diagonal-corner technique to make one each of units 5 and 6. Make two each of units 8 and 13.

2. Use diagonal-corner technique to make two of Unit 2. Note that the second unit is a mirror image, so refer to diagram carefully to position pieces correctly.

3. Use diagonal-corner technique to make four of Unit 12. Note that two units are mirror images.

4. Use diagonal-end technique to make two of Unit 4. The second unit is a mirror image.

Block C Assembly

Assemble this block in vertical sections X and Y. Refer to Block C Assembly Diagram throughout to identify units. Each completed block should measure approximately 10¼" x 14".

Section X

1. Join both pair of units 3 and 4 as shown.

2. Join units 1, 2, and 3/4 in two vertical rows as shown.

3. Join units 5 and 6.

4. Sew units 1/2/3/4 to sides of unit 5/6.

5. Join Unit 7 to bottom of combined unit.

6. Sew Unit 9 to one of Unit 10.

7. Join Unit 8 to sides of unit 9/10. Sew 8/9/10 to bottom of Unit 7.

Section Y

1. Referring to left side of diagram, join units 10, 11, 12, and 13 in a vertical row as shown.

2. For right side of block, join remaining units 10, 11, 12, and 13 in a row as shown.

Assembly

Join Y sections to sides of Section X to complete block. Make seven of Block B.

Units for Block D

Refer to Block D Assembly Diagram throughout to identify units.

1. Referring Strip Set 1 Diagram, join ⅞"-wide strips of Fabric II to both sides of 1¼"-wide strip of Fabric VI. Make two of Strip Set 1. From these, cut thirty-eight 1¼"-wide segments for Unit 1.

Strip Set 1—Make 2.

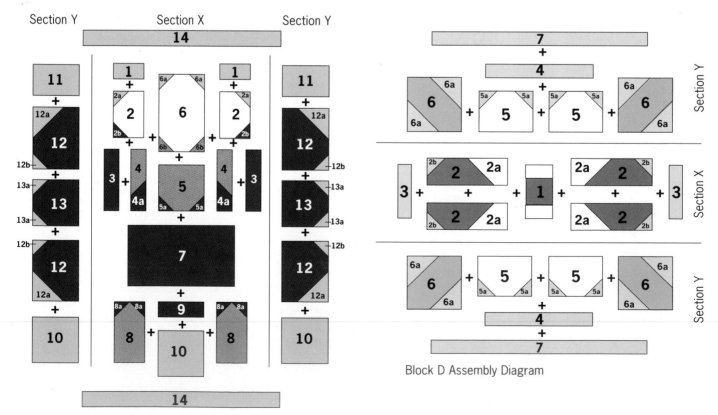

Block C Assembly Diagram

Block D Assembly Diagram

2. Use diagonal-end technique to sew piece 2a to piece 2. Complete Unit 2 by adding diagonal corner 2b as shown. Make another of Unit 2 in same manner; then make two mirror-image units.

3. Use diagonal-corner technique to make four each of units 5 and 6.

Block D Assembly

This block is assembled in horizontal sections X and Y. Refer to Block D Assembly Diagram throughout to identify units. Each completed block should measure approximately 5¾" x 6½".

Section X

1. Join mirror-image Unit 2s in pairs as shown.

2. Join Unit 2 pairs to opposite sides of Unit 1.

3. Sew a Unit 3 to each end of combined unit.

Section Y

1. Referring to top of assembly diagram, join two of Unit 5.

2. Sew Unit 4 to top of combined Unit 5s.

3. Join a Unit 6 to each end of 4/5 unit.

4. Make bottom Y section in same manner.

Assembly

Join Y sections to Section X. Sew Unit 7 to top and bottom edges to complete block. Make 38 of Block D.   *(continued)*

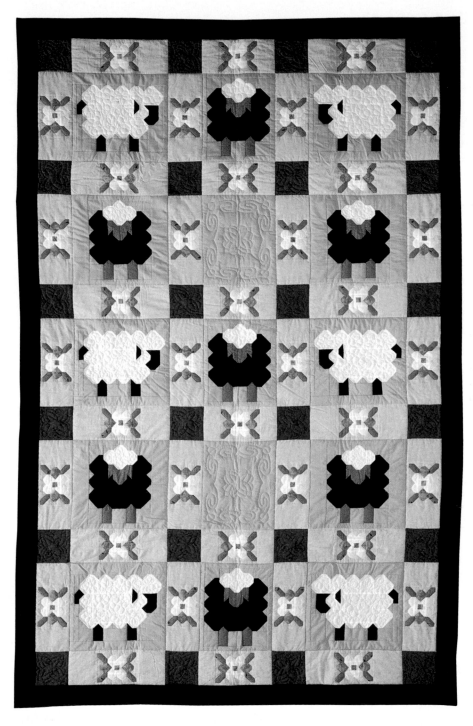

Quilt Assembly

Refer to Row Assembly Diagram for placement of blocks in rows. Assemble each row from left to right.

Row 1

1. Select one each of blocks A, B, and C. Also select four of Block D, two of Spacer F, and eight of Sashing 2.
2. To make sashing units, join Sashing 2 to opposite sides of each D block.
3. Sew Spacer F to sides of Block C.
4. Join blocks and sashing units in a horizontal row as shown.
5. Make three of Row 1.

Sashing Row

1. Select three of Block D, four of Sashing 3, two of Sashing 1 and four Fabric VIII sashing squares.
2. To make sashing units, join Sashing 3 to opposite sides of two D blocks. Join Sashing 1 to sides of remaining D block.
3. Join sashing units and squares in a horizontal row as shown.
4. Make six Sashing Rows.

Row 2

1. Select two C blocks, four D blocks, four of Spacer G, and eight of Sashing 2.
2. Join Sashing 2 to opposite sides of each D block.
3. Sew Spacer G to sides of both C blocks.
4. Join blocks and sashing units in a horizontal row as shown.
5. Make two of Row 2.

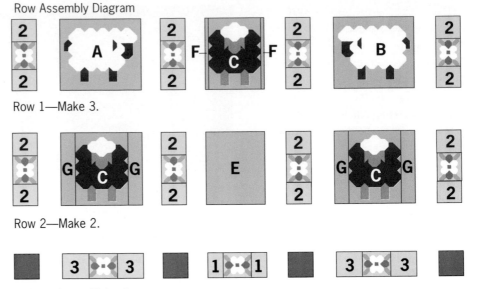

Row Assembly Diagram

Row 1—Make 3.

Row 2—Make 2.

Sashing Row—Make 6.

Assembly

1. Referring to photo, lay out rows. Start with a Sashing Row and alternate rows 1 and 2 with sashing rows between them.
2. When satisfied with row placement, join rows.

Borders

1. Join three Fabric I strips end-to-end for each side border. Join two strips for top and bottom borders.
2. Referring to instructions on page 17, measure quilt from top to bottom. Measuring outward from center of border strips, trim side borders to match length. Matching centers, sew borders to quilt sides.
3. Measure quilt from side to side; then trim remaining borders to match quilt width. Sew borders to top and bottom edges. Press seam allowances toward border.

Quilting and Finishing

1. Mark quilting design on quilt top as desired. On quilt shown, patchwork is outline-quilted, with additional swirls quilted in the sheep bodies to represent wooly fleece. Use a stencil to mark a design of your choice in spacer blocks.
2. Divide backing into two 3¼-yard lengths. Cut one piece in half lengthwise. Join one narrow panel to both sides of wide piece to assemble backing.
3. Layer backing, batting, and quilt top. Baste. Quilt as marked or as desired.
4. From Fabric I strips, make 10 yards of straight-grain binding. See page 22 for instructions on making and applying binding.

Crows *in the* Corn

*When the corn is as high as an elephant's eye, it's picnic time.
Dress your table for a summer feast with this patchwork tablecloth that's full of
charm. If you like things corny, add wider borders to make a twin-sized quilt.*

Finished Size

Tablecloth: 56" x 83"
Blocks: 36 crow blocks, 4" x 4½"
6 corn blocks, 6" x 16"

Materials

	Fabric I (white solid)	3⅜ yards
	Fabric II (green check)	2¼ yards
	Fabric III (gold print)	½ yard
	Fabric IV (yellow solid)	⅜ yard
	Fabric V (black solid)	½ yard
	Fabric VI (gray print)	⅜ yard
	90"-wide backing fabric	1¾ yards
	Low-loft batting (optional)	72" x 90"
	Gold embroidery floss	1 skein

Quick-Piecing Techniques

Strip Piecing (see page 12)
Diagonal Corners (see page 12)
Diagonal Ends (see page 13)

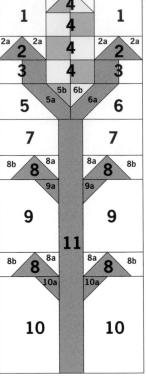

Block A—Make 6.

Cutting

Cut all strips crossgrain, from selvage to selvage. For best use of yardage, cut pieces in order listed. Refer to diagrams to identify pieces.

From Fabric I (white solid), cut:

* One 16½"-wide strip. From this, cut:
  • One 16½" x 33½" (M).
  • Two 5½" x 6½" (I).
* One 10½"-wide strip. From this, cut:
  • Four 10½" squares (D1).
* Two 9½"-wide strips. From these, cut:
  • Four 9½" x 13½" (H).
  • Four 4½" x 9½" (G).
* One 8½"-wide strip. From this, cut:
  • Two 8½" x 21½" (L).
* Three 4½"-wide strips. From these, cut:
  • Two 4½" x 11½" (K).
  • Eight 4½" squares (E).
  • Twelve 3" x 4½" (A10).
  • Twelve 1" x 4½" (F).

* Four 3½"-wide strips. From these, cut:
  • Thirty-six 3½" squares (B4, C4).
  • Thirty-six 1" x 3½" (B1, C1).
* One 3"-wide strip. From this, cut:
  • Twelve 3" x 3½" (A9).
* Three 2½"-wide strips. Set aside two strips for Strip Set 3. From remaining strip, cut:
  • Two 2½" x 3½" (J).
  • Twelve 2½" squares (A1).
* Two 2¼"-wide strips for Strip Set 3.
* Three 2"-wide strips. From these, cut:
  • Twenty-four 2" x 3" (A5, A6, A7).
  • Twenty-four 1½" x 2" (A8b).
* Six 1½"-wide strips. Set aside two strips for strip sets 1 and 4. From remaining strips, cut:
  • Ninety-six 1½" squares (A2a, A4a, A8a, B2a, C2a).
* Two ¾"-wide strips for Strip Set 3.

From Fabric II (green check), cut:

* Eight 4½"-wide strips for Borders 1 and 2.
* Seven 3"-wide strips for binding.

* One 2"-wide strip. From this, cut:
  • Twelve 2" x 2½" (A5a, A6a).
* Six 1½"-wide strips. Set aside one strip for Strip Set 1. From remaining strips, cut:
  • Six 1½" x 11" (A11).
  • Thirty-six 1½" x 2½" (A2, A8).
  • Twenty-four 1½" squares (A9a, A10a).

From Fabric III (gold print), cut:

* Six 1½"-wide strips. Set aside five strips for strip sets 2 and 4. From remaining strip, cut:
  • Six 1½" squares (A5b).
  • Thirty-six 1" squares (B1a, C1a). *Note:* If necessary, cut two or three squares from strip for Strip Set 4.
* Four ¾"-wide strips for Strip Set 3.

From Fabric IV (yellow solid), cut:

* Five 1½"-wide strips. Set aside four strips for Strip Set 2. From remaining strip, cut:
  • Six 1½" squares (A6b).

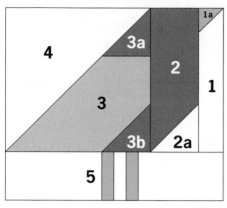

Block B—Make 18.

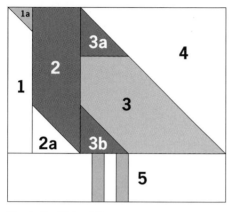

Block C—Make 18.

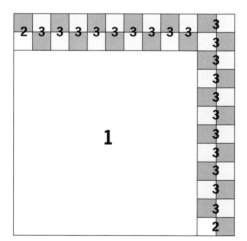

Block D—Make 4.

From Fabric V (black solid), cut:

✶ Eight 1½"-wide strips. From these, cut:
   • Seventy-two 1½" x 3½" (B2, B3a, C2, C3a).
   • Thirty-six 1½" squares (B3b, C3b).

From Fabric VI (gray print), cut:

✶ Three 2½"-wide strips. From these, cut:
   • Thirty-six 2½" x 3½" (B3, C3).

Units for Block A

Refer to strip set diagrams and Block A Assembly Diagram throughout to identify units.

1. For Strip Set 1, join 1½"-wide strips of fabrics I and II. Press seam allowances toward Fabric II. From this strip set, cut twelve 1½"-wide segments for Unit 3.

2. For Strip Set 2, join 1½"-wide strips of fabrics III and IV. Make four strip sets. Press seam allowances toward Fabric III. From these strip sets, cut twenty-four 1½"-wide segments for Unit 4. Set aside remainder for Block D.

3. Use diagonal-corner technique to add 4a corners to one Unit 4 segment.

4. Use diagonal-corner technique to make two each of units 2, 9, and 10.

5. Use diagonal-end technique to join 5a to piece 5. Then add diagonal corner 5b. Make Unit 6 in same manner, making sure angle of diagonal end is a mirror image of Unit 5.

6. Join diagonal end 8b to two of Unit 8; then add diagonal corner 8a. Make two more of Unit 8 that are mirror-image units, with angles of diagonal ends and diagonal corners opposite those of first pair.

Block A Assembly

Assemble this block in two sections. Each completed section should measure approximately 6½" wide. Refer to Block A Assembly Diagram throughout.

Section X

1. For each side of this section, join units 1, 2, and 3 in a row.

2. Join four of Unit 4 in a vertical row as shown, placing unit with corners at top.

3. Sew 1/2/3 units to sides of Unit 4 row.

4. Join units 5 and 6.

5. Sew unit 5/6 to bottom of combined 1/2/3/4 unit.

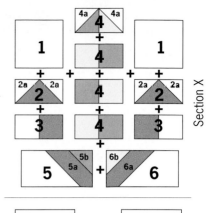

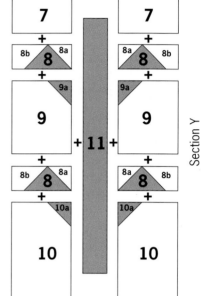

Block A Assembly Diagram

Strip Set 1—Make 1.

Strip Set 2—Make 4.

Section Y

1. Join units 7, 8, 9, and 10 in a row for each side of block. Position mirror-image Unit 8s as shown.

2. Sew combined units to both sides of Unit 11.

Assembly

Join sections X and Y to complete corn block. Make six of Block A.

(continued)

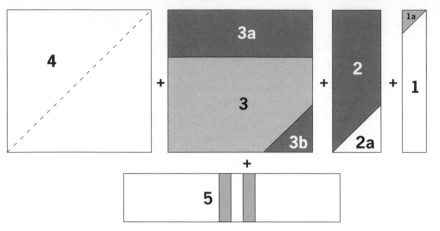

Block B Assembly Diagram

Units for Block B

Refer to strip set diagrams and Block B Assembly Diagram throughout to identify units.

1. For Strip Set 3, join ¾"-wide strips of fabrics I and III as shown. Then join 2¼"-wide and 2½"-wide strips of Fabric I to top and bottom edges. Make two strip sets. Press seam allowances away from center. From these strip sets, cut thirty-six 1½"-wide segments for Unit 5.

2. Use diagonal-corner technique to make one each of units 1 and 2.

3. Join strip 3a to one edge of piece 3 as shown. Use diagonal-corner technique to add 3b.

Block B Assembly

1. Join units 1, 2, and 3 in a row as shown.

2. Use diagonal-corner technique to sew Unit 4 to left end of row.

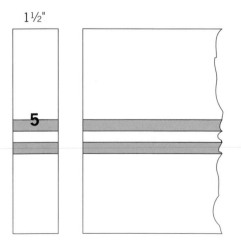

Strip Set 3—Make 2.

Press; then trim excess fabric from seam allowance.

3. Add Unit 5 to bottom of block, positioning wider Fabric I strip under Unit 3.

4. Make 18 of Block B.

Block C Assembly

Block C is a mirror image of Block B. Units are the same, but diagonal corners are reversed. Referring to block diagram, make 18 of Block C.

Block D Assembly

Block D is the corner of the table-cloth. Each completed block should measure approximately 12½" square.

1. For Strip Set 4, join 1½"-wide strips of fabrics I and III. From this strip set, cut eight 1½"-wide segments for Unit 2. Cut and set aside four more segments for tablecloth assembly.

2. From remainder of Strip Set 2, cut eighty 1½"-wide segments for Unit 3. Cut and set aside two more segments for tablecloth assembly.

3. Join nine of Unit 3 in a row, alternating fabrics as shown (Block D Assembly Diagram). Add one Unit 2 to left end of row. Join row to square D1.

4. Join 11 of Unit 3 in a row as shown, adding one Unit 2 to bottom of row. Join row to adjacent side of D1 as shown.

5. Make four of Block D.

Tablecloth Assembly

Assemble the tablecloth in three sections—two of Section X and one of Section Y. Refer to bottom half of Tablecloth Assembly Diagram to assemble sections (top half is the same, but upside-down).

Section X

1. Join two B blocks side-by-side.

2. Sew one E and one F to sides of another B block.

3. Sew E/B/F row to top edge of joined B blocks.

4. Sew G to top edge of combined unit.

5. Join assembled unit to one side of Block D as shown.

6. Repeat steps 1 and 2 to join three C blocks. Sew combined C blocks to one side of H.

7. Join both units as shown to complete corner.

8. Repeat steps 1–7 to make another corner in same manner.

9. Join I to top of Block A.

10. Sew corners to both sides of A/I unit.

11. Repeat to make second Section X.

Strip Set 4—Make 1.

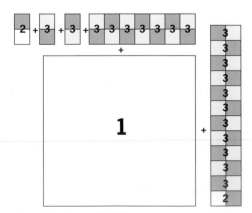

Block D Assembly Diagram

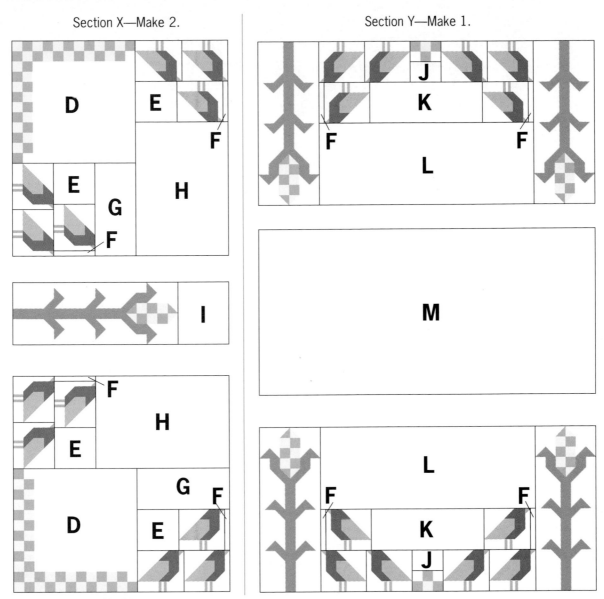

Section X—Make 2.

Section Y—Make 1.

Tablecloth Assembly Diagram

Section Y

1. Join two Strip Set 4 segments to sides of one Strip Set 2 segment as shown. Add J to top of combined segments.

2. Join two B blocks; then join two C blocks. Sew each pair to sides of J unit as shown.

3. Sew one C block and one B block to both ends of K. Add Fs to both ends of row as shown.

4. Join both assembled rows as shown. Then sew L to top edge.

5. Add an A block to both sides of center unit.

6. Repeat steps 1–5 to make a second center unit.

7. Sew center units to both sides of M.

Assembly

Sew one Section X to both sides of Section Y.

Borders

1. For each border, join two 4½"-wide strips of Fabric II end-to-end.

2. Referring to instructions on page 17, measure length of tablecloth. Trim two borders to match length. Sew these to long sides of tablecloth.

3. Measure width of tablecloth. Measuring from center seam, trim remaining border to match width. Sew borders to shorter edges of tablecloth. Press seam allowances toward borders.

Quilting and Finishing

1. Mark quilting design on quilt top as desired. On tablecloth shown, patchwork is outline-quilted. If desired, draw curls of wavy corn silk at top of each ear of corn.

2. Layer backing and quilt top (low-loft batting is optional for tablecloth). Baste. Quilt as marked or as desired.

3. Use two strands of embroidery floss to quilt corn silk.

4. From Fabric II strips, make eight yards of straight-grain binding. See page 22 for instructions on making and applying binding.

Intersection

Strip piecing combines with log cabin-type construction to make this project. Chains of dark squares march in diagonal rows across the surface of this quilt, marked with nine-patch blocks at each junction.

Finished Size
Quilt: 69" x 99"
Blocks: 24 blocks, 12" square

Quick-Piecing Technique
Strip Piecing (see page 12)

Materials

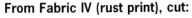

▢	Fabric I (ivory print)	2⅝ yards
▢	Fabric II (blue solid)	2⅞ yards
▢	Fabric III (tan-and-blue print)	2¾ yards
▢	Fabric IV (rust print)	1½ yards
	Backing fabric	6 yards
	Precut batting	90" x 108"

Cutting

Cut all strips crossgrain, from selvage to selvage. For best use of yardage, cut pieces in order listed. Refer to diagrams to identify pieces.

From Fabric I (ivory print), cut:
* Sixteen 3½"-wide strips. Set aside five strips for strip sets 1 and 2. From remaining strips, cut:
  * Four 3½" x 24½" (Sashing Strip E).
  * Three 3½" x 21½" (Sashing Strip D).
  * Twenty-four 3½" x 9½" (Sashing Strip C).
* Nine 2"-wide strips for inner border.
* Seven 1½"-wide strips for strip sets 3 and 4.

From Fabric II (blue solid), cut:
* Four 3½"-wide strips. Set aside three strips for Strip Set 2. From remaining strip, cut:
  * Eight 3½" sashing squares.
* Nine 3"-wide strips for binding.
* Eight 1½"-wide strips for strip sets 3 and 4.
* Twenty 2"-wide strips for second and outer borders.

From Fabric III (tan print), cut:
* Forty-seven 1½"-wide strips. Set aside six strips for Strip Set 5. From remaining strips, cut:
  * Thirty-two 1½" x 11½" (A12, A13).
  * Thirty-two 1½" x 9½" (A14a, B8, B11b).
  * Thirty-two 1½" x 8½" (A8, B7, B11a).
  * Sixty-four 1½" x 7½" (A4, A5, A9a, B4, B9b).
  * Thirty-two 1½" x 6½" (A3, B3, B9a).
* Nine 2"-wide strips for third border.

From Fabric IV (rust print), cut:
* Two 3½"-wide strips for Strip Set 1.
* Twenty-four 1½"-wide strips. Set aside three strips for Strip Set 5. From remaining strips, cut:
  * Thirty-two 1½" x 9½" (A7, A10).
  * Thirty-two 1½" x 8½" (A11a, B6, B10b).
  * Thirty-two 1½" x 7½" (A6, B5, B10a).

(continued)

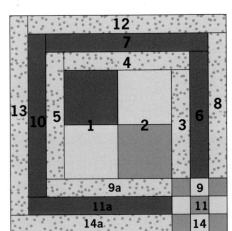

Block A—Make 16.

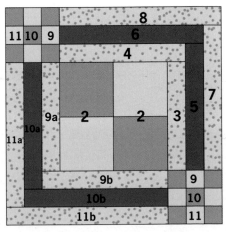

Block B—Make 8.

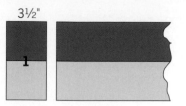

3½"

9 14 9 11

Strip Set 1—Make 2.

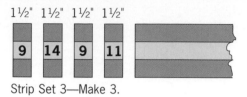

1½" 1½" 1½" 1½"

Strip Set 3—Make 3.

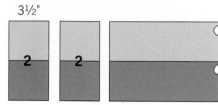

3½"

2 2

Strip Set 2—Make 3.

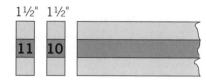

1½" 1½"

11 10

Strip Set 4—Make 2.

Strip Piecing for Blocks A and B

Refer to strip-set diagrams and block assembly diagrams to identify units. Store strip-set segments in labelled zip-top bags.

1. For Strip Set 1, join 3½"-wide strips of fabrics I and IV as shown. Make two of Strip Set 1. Press seam allowances toward Fabric IV. From these strip sets, cut sixteen 3½"-wide segments for Unit A1.

2. For Strip Set 2, join 3½"-wide strips of fabrics I and II as shown. Make three of Strip Set 2. Press seam allowances toward Fabric II. From these strip sets, cut thirty-two 3½"-wide segments for units A2 and B2.

3. For Strip Set 3, join 1½"-wide strips of fabrics I and II as shown. Make three of Strip Set 3. Press seam allowances toward Fabric II. From these strip sets, cut sixty-four 1½"-wide segments for units A9, A14, B9, and B11.

4. For Strip Set 4, join 1½"-wide strips of fabrics I and II as shown. Make two of Strip Set 4. Press seam allowances toward Fabric II. From these strip sets, cut thirty-two 1½"-wide segments for units A11 and B10.

Block A Assembly

Assemble this block from the center out. Each completed block should measure approximately 12½" square. Refer to Block A Assembly Diagram throughout.

1. Join units in numerical order as shown. Work around block to Unit 8. As strips are added, press seam allowances toward strip just added.

2. Join Unit 9 to 9a. Press seam allowance toward 9a. Join combined Unit 9 to bottom of block.

3. Add Unit 10 to left side of block as shown.

4. Join Unit 11 to 11a. Press seam allowances toward Unit 11. Join combined Unit 11 to bottom of block.

5. Add units 12 and 13 as shown.

6. Join Unit 14 to 14a. Press seam allowances toward 14a. Join combined Unit 14 to bottom of block.

7. Make 16 of Block A.

Block B Assembly

Make Block B in the same manner as for Block A. Referring to Block B Assembly Diagram, join units 2–11 in numerical order as shown. As strips are added, press seam allowances toward strip just added. Make eight of Block B.

(continued)

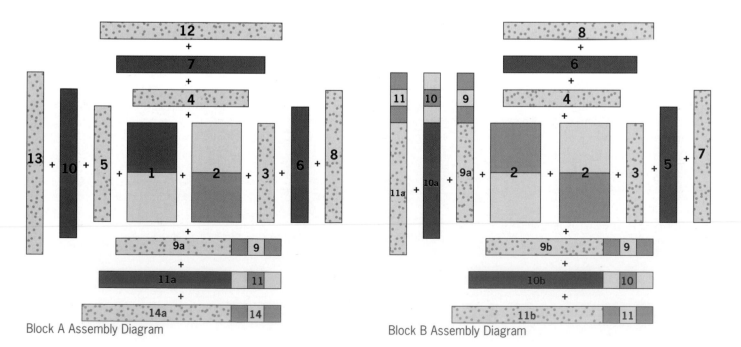

Block A Assembly Diagram

Block B Assembly Diagram

Quilt Assembly

Make sashing units as described below. Refer to Row Assembly Diagram for placement of blocks and sashing units in rows.

1. For Strip Set 5, join 1½"-wide strips of fabrics III and IV as shown. Make three of Strip Set 5. Press seam allowances toward Fabric IV. From these strip sets, cut thirty-four 3½"-wide segments for sashing units.

3½"

Strip Set 5—Make 3.

Sashing Unit—Make 24.

Row Assembly Diagram

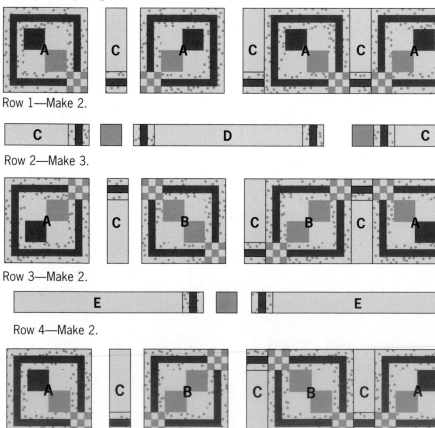

Row 1—Make 2.

Row 2—Make 3.

Row 3—Make 2.

Row 4—Make 2.

Row 5—Make 2.

2. Referring to Sashing Unit Diagram, sew one segment from Strip Set 5 to one end of each C and E sashing strip. Sew a segment to both ends of each D strip.

3. For Row 1, select four A blocks and three C sashing units. Positioning nine-patch corner of each block as shown, join blocks and sashing in a row. Make two of Row 1.

4. For Row 2, select two Cs, 1 D, and two Fabric II sashing squares. Join units in a row as shown. Make three of Row 2.

5. For Row 3, select two each of blocks A and B, and three C units. Join blocks and sashing as shown. Make two of Row 3.

6. For Row 4, join two E sashing units and one sashing square as shown. Make two of Row 4.

7. For Row 5, select two A blocks, two B blocks, and three C units. Join blocks and sashing as shown. Make two of Row 5.

8. Join rows 1–5 in numerical order to assemble half the quilt. Join second set of rows 1–5 in same manner. Referring to photo on page 71, turn second half upside down. Join halves with remaining Row 2 between them.

Borders

1. For Fabric I inner border, cut one strip in half. For each side border, join a strip to both ends of each short piece. For top and bottom borders, join two strips end-to-end.

2. Referring to instructions on page 17, measure quilt from top to bottom. Trim longer borders to match quilt length. Sew borders to quilt sides. Press seam allowances toward borders.

3. Measure quilt from side to side. Trim remaining borders to match width. Sew borders to top and bottom edges of quilt.

4. For second border, repeat steps 1–3 with Fabric II strips.

5. For third border, join three Fabric III strips end-to-end for each side and two strips for top and bottom borders. Measure and sew borders to quilt as before.

6. For outer border, repeat Step 5 with Fabric II strips.

Quilting and Finishing

1. Mark quilting design on quilt top as desired. On quilt shown, patchwork is outline-quilted.

2. Divide backing into two 3-yard lengths. Cut one piece in half lengthwise. Join one narrow panel to each side of wide piece to assemble backing.

3. Layer backing, batting, and quilt top. Baste. Quilt as marked or as desired.

4. From Fabric II strips, make 9¾ yards of straight-grain binding. See page 22 for instructions on making and applying binding.

Old Bones

The king of dinosaurs, Tyrannosaurus Rex, roars for attention on this colorful quilt that's sure to please young paleontologists. If your child is thrilled by Godzilla, he'll love blue Brachiosaurus and green Triceratops. Quick piecing lets you sew with speed, make no bones about it!

Finished Size

Quilt: 65½" x 93½"
Blocks: 15 dinosaur blocks, 15½" x 16½"
16 bone blocks, 4" x 16½"

Quick-Piecing Techniques

Diagonal Corners (see page 12)
Diagonal Ends (see page 13)

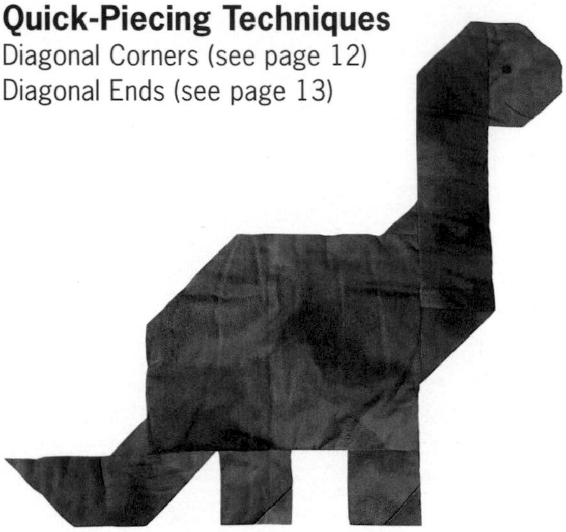

Materials

☐	Fabric I (white solid)	2⅛ yards
■	Fabric II (blue-green print)	1¾ yards
▨	Fabric III (light blue solid)	1½ yards
■	Fabric IV (dark green print)	⅜ yard
▨	Fabric V (bright green solid)	¾ yard
■	Fabric VI (orange print)	1¼ yards
	Fabric VII (blue-green dot)	1⅛ yards
	Backing fabric	5¾ yards
	Precut batting	81" x 96"
	Fine-tipped black fabric marker (optional)	

Cutting

Cut all strips crossgrain, from selvage to selvage. For best use of yardage, cut pieces in order listed. In some cases, you'll need to trim a strip to a narrower width to cut remaining pieces listed or use fabric left over from cutting larger pieces. Refer to block diagrams to identify pieces.

From Fabric I (white), cut:

✱ One 17"-wide strip. From this, cut:
  - Sixteen 1¼" x 17" (A12, B12, E15, F15).
  - Two 11" squares (E1, F1).
  - Six 3" x 5½" (A10, B10).
  - Two 1½" x 5½" (E13, F13).

✱ Two 6½"-wide strips. From these, cut:
  - Six 6½" x 8" (A2, B2).
  - Two 6½" x 7" (E12, F12).
  - Two 2" x 3½" (E9, F9).
  - Six 1" x 3½" (A8, B8).
  - Six 3" squares (A3a, B3a).

✱ Three 5"-wide strips. From these, cut:
  - Six 5" x 12½" (A1, B1).
  - Six 5" x 6½" (A11, B11).
  - Two 2" x 4½" (E3b, F3b).
  - Two 1½" x 3½" (E7, F7).

✱ Two 2½"-wide strips. From these, cut:
  - Two 2½" x 9" (E4, F4).
  - Six 2½" x 3" (A6b, B6b).
  - Six 2½" squares (A6a, B6a).
  - Eight 2" x 2½" (A4, B4, E3a, F3a).
  - Two 1" x 2½" (E5, F5).

✱ Three 2"-wide strips. From these and scraps, cut:
  - Eight 2" squares (A7a, B7a, E11a, F11a).
  - Sixty-four 1¾" x 2" (G2).

✱ Seven 1½"-wide strips. From these, cut:
  - Sixteen 1½" x 10" (G4).
  - Four 1½" x 2" (E8a, E10a, F9a, F10a).
  - Eighty 1½" squares (A9a, B9a, E2a, E6a, F2a, F6a, G3a).

From Fabric II (blue-green), cut:

✱ One 8"-wide strip. From this, cut:
  - Six 6½" x 8" (A3, B3).

✱ Three 2¾"-wide strips. From these, cut:
  - Thirty-two 2¾" x 3½" (G1).

✱ Four 2½"-wide strips. From these, cut:
  - Six 2½" x 8½" (A7, B7).
  - Six 2½" x 6½" (A6, B6).
  - Six 2½" x 3½" (A9, B9).
  - Eighteen 2½" squares (A5, A11a, B5, B11a).

✱ Nine 1½"-wide strips. From these and scraps, cut:
  - Thirty-two 1½" x 10" (G3).
  - Fourteen 1½" squares (A1a, A2a, B1a, B2a, E13a, F13a).

✱ Sixteen 1"-wide strips. From these, cut:
  - Thirty-two 1" x 17" (G5).
  - 128 1" squares (G2a).

From Fabric III (light blue), cut:

✱ One 8¾"-wide strip. From this, cut:
  - Seven 5" x 8¾" (C10, D10).
  - Seven 1" x 7" (C2, D2).

✱ One 6½"-wide strip. From this, cut:
  - Seven 4¾" x 6½" (C7, D7).

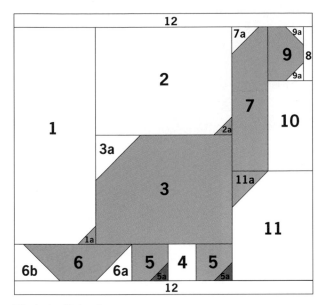

Block A—Make 3.

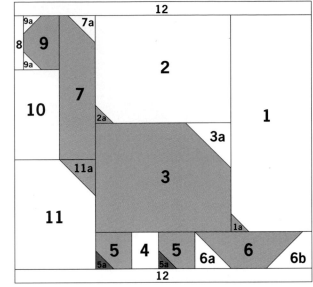

Block B—Make 3.

* Four 3¾"-wide strips. From these, cut:
  • Seven 3¾" x 17" (C16, D16).
  • Seven 3¾" x 4½" (C4, D4).
* Five 2½"-wide strips. From these, cut:
  • Seven 2½" x 6¼" (C1, D1).
  • Fourteen 2½" x 3" (C12, C15a, D12, D15a).
  • Thirty-five 2½" squares (C5a, C11, C13, C15b, D5a, D11, D13, D15b).
* One 2"-wide strip. From this, cut:
  • Seven 2" x 4" (C3b, D3b).
  • Seven 2" squares (C3a, D3a).
* From scraps, cut:
  • Seven 3" squares (C9a, D9a).

From Fabric IV (dark green), cut:
* Three 2½"-wide strips. From these, cut:
  • Seven 2½" x 6½" (C8, D8).
  • Seven 2½" x 4½" (C5, D5).
  • Fourteen 2½" squares (C6a, C12a, D6a, D12a).
* One 1½"-wide strip. From this, cut:
  • Twenty-eight 1½" squares (C6b, C7a, C14a, D6b, D7a, D14a).

From Fabric V (bright green), cut:
* Three 4½"-wide strips. From these, cut:
  • Seven 4½" x 6½" (C9, D9).
  • Seven 4½" x 5½" (C6, D6).
  • Fourteen 1½" squares (C8b, C11a, D8b, D11a).
* Three 2½"-wide strips. From these, cut:
  • Seven 2½" x 6½" (C15, D15).
  • Twenty-one 2½" squares (C8a, C14, D8a, D14).
  • Seven 2" x 5" (C3, D3).

(continued)

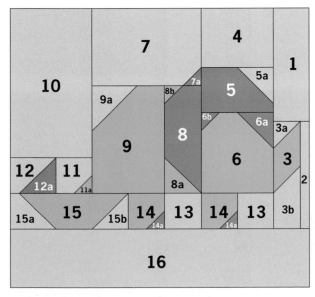

Block C—Make 4.

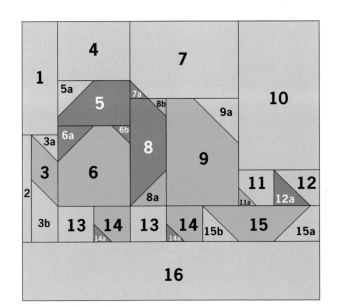

Block D—Make 3.

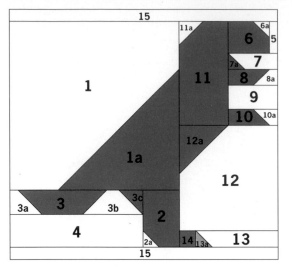

Block E—Make 1.

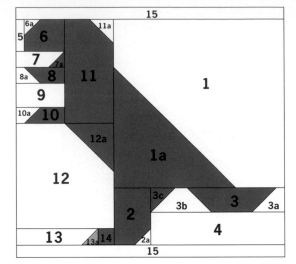

Block F—Make 1.

From Fabric VI (orange), cut:

✱ One 8"-wide strip. From this, cut:
- Two 8" squares (E1a, F1a).
- One 4½" x 26" strip and one 3½" x 26" strip. From these, cut:
  - Four 4½" squares for border corners.
  - Two 3½" x 7" (E11, F11).
  - Two 3½" squares (E12a, F12a).
  - Sixteen 1½" squares (A5a, B5a, E7a, E14, F7a, F14).

✱ One 2½"-wide strip. From this, cut:
- Two 2½" x 4" (E2, F2).
- Two 2½" x 3" (E6, F6).
- Two 2" x 6" (E3, F3).
- Two 2" squares (E3c, F3c).
- Four 1½" x 3" (E8, E10, F8, F10).

✱ Eight 3"-wide strips for binding.

From Fabric VII (blue-green dot), cut:

✱ Eight 4½"-wide strips for borders.

Units for Block A

Refer to Block A Assembly Diagram throughout to identify units.

1. Use diagonal-corner technique to make two of Unit 5 and one each of units 1, 2, 3, 7, 9, and 11.

2. Use diagonal-corner technique to add 6a to Unit 6 and diagonal-end technique to add 6b.

Block A Assembly

Assemble this block in sections X and Y. Refer to Block A Assembly Diagram throughout.

1. Join units 2 and 3. Add Unit 1 to side of combined units.

2. Join units 4, 5, and 6 in a row as shown.

3. Sew 4/5/6 row to bottom of 1/2/3 unit to complete Section X.

4. Join units 8 and 9. Add Unit 10 to bottom of 8/9 unit.

5. Sew Unit 7 to side of 8/9/10 unit.

6. Sew Unit 11 to bottom to complete Section Y.

7. Join sections X and Y.

8. Sew Unit 12 to top and bottom edges of block.

9. Make three of Block A.

Block B Assembly

Block B is a mirror image of Block A. Make units in the same manner, but reverse angles of diagonal end and diagonal corners. Referring to Block B Diagram, make three of Block B.

Units for Block C

Refer to Block C Assembly Diagram throughout to identify units.

1. Use diagonal-corner technique to make two of Unit 14 and one each of units 5, 6, 7, 8, 9, 11, and 12.

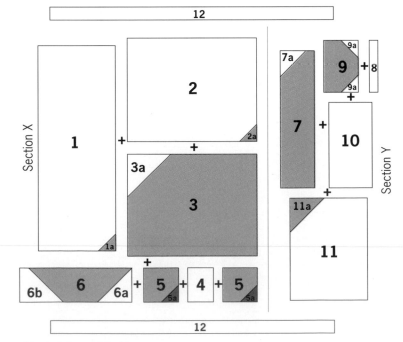

Block A Assembly Diagram

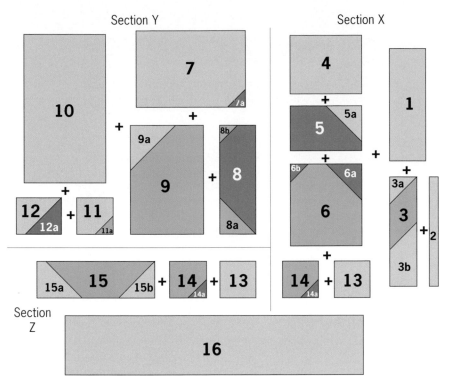

Block C Assembly Diagram

Block D Assembly

Block D is a mirror image of Block C. Make units in the same manner, but reverse angles of diagonal corners. Referring to Block D Diagram, make three of Block D.

Units for Block E

Refer to Block E Assembly Diagram throughout to identify units.

1. Use diagonal-corner technique to make one each of units 1, 2, 6, 7, 11, 12, and 13.

2. Use diagonal-end technique to make one each of units 8 and 10.

3. For Unit 3, use diagonal-end technique to add 3a and 3b to sides of Unit 3. Use diagonal-corner technique to add 3c to 3b.

2. Use diagonal-end technique and diagonal-corner technique to make one each of units 3 and 15.

Block C Assembly

Assemble this block in sections X, Y, and Z. Refer to Block C Assembly Diagram throughout.

Section X

1. Join units 2 and 3. Then add Unit 1 to top of 2/3 unit.

2. Join one each of units 13 and 14. Then join units 4, 5, 6, and 13/14 in a row as shown.

3. Join both rows to complete Section X.

Section Y

1. Join units 8 and 9. Then add Unit 7 to top of 8/9 unit.

2. Join units 11 and 12. Then add Unit 10 to top of 11/12 unit.

3. Join 7/8/9 unit and 10/11/12 unit to complete Section Y.

Section Z

Join units 13, 14, and 15 in a row as shown.

Assembly

1. Join Section Z to bottom of Section Y.

2. Sew Section X to right side of block.

3. Add Unit 16 to bottom to complete block.

4. Make four of Block C.

Block E Assembly

Assemble this block in sections X and Y. Refer to Block E Assembly Diagram throughout.

Section X

1. Join units 3 and 4. Then sew Unit 2 to side of 3/4 unit.

2. Sew Unit 1 to top of 2/3/4 unit.

(continued)

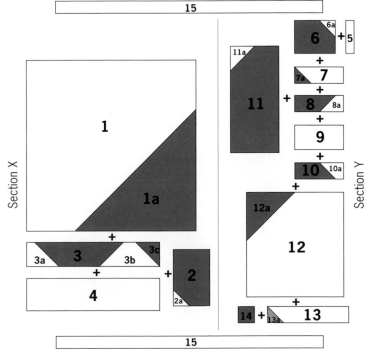

Block E Assembly Diagram

Section Y

1. Join units 5 and 6.

2. Join units 5/6, 7, 8, 9, and 10 in a row as shown.

3. Sew Unit 11 to side of combined row as shown.

4. Add Unit 12 to bottom of combined units.

5. Join units 13 and 14. Sew 13/14 to bottom of Unit 12.

Assembly

1. Join sections X and Y.

2. Sew Unit 15 to top and bottom of block.

3. Make one of Block E.

Block F Assembly

Block F is a mirror image of Block E. Make units in the same manner, but reverse angles of diagonal corners. Referring to Block F Diagram, make one of Block F.

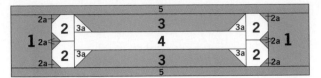

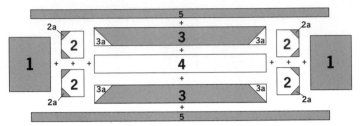

Block G—Make 16.

Block G Assembly Diagram

Block G Assembly

Refer to Block G Assembly Diagram throughout.

1. Use diagonal-corner technique to make four of Unit 2 and two Unit 3.

2. Join units 3 and 4 as shown.

3. Join two of Unit 2. Sew combined units to one side of 3/4 unit as shown. Join second pair of Unit 2s in same manner and join to opposite side of 3/4 unit.

4. Sew Unit 1 to both ends of block as shown.

5. Sew Unit 5 to top and bottom of block.

6. Make 16 of Block G.

Quilt Assembly

Refer to photo and Row Assembly Diagram for placement of blocks in each row.

1. If desired, use fine-tipped marker to draw smiles and dots for eyes on each dinosaur before assembly.

2. For Row 1, join three G blocks and two border corners as shown. Make two of Row 1.

3. Trim ½" from both short sides of remaining G blocks to get ten 4½" x 16" bone blocks for remaining rows.

4. For Row 2, join one each of blocks A, B, and C as shown. Sew G blocks to both sides of row. Make two of Row 2 as shown. Then make another row, putting a D block in place of C.

5. For Row 3, join one each of blocks C, D, and E as shown. Sew G blocks to both sides of row. Make one of Row 4 as shown. Then make another row, putting an F block in place of E.

6. Referring to photo, join rows in 1-2-3-2-3-2-1 sequence.

Row Assembly Diagram

Row 1—Make 2.

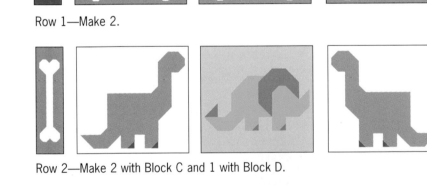

Row 2—Make 2 with Block C and 1 with Block D.

Row 3—Make 1 with Block E and 1 with Block F.

Borders

1. For borders, trim a 7"-long piece from ends of two Fabric VII border strips. For each side border, join a full-length strip to both ends of a 7" piece. For top and bottom borders, join two 35"-long strips.

2. Referring to instructions on page 17, measure quilt from top to bottom. Measuring from center, trim longer border strips to match length. Sew borders to quilt sides.

3. Measure quilt from side to side; then trim remaining borders to match quilt width. Sew borders to top and bottom edges of quilt. Press seam allowances toward borders.

Quilting and Finishing

1. Mark quilting design on quilt top as desired. On quilt shown, patchwork is outline-quilted. The background of each block is machine stipple-quilted.

2. Divide backing into two 2⅞-yard lengths. Cut one piece in half lengthwise. Join one narrow panel to each side of wide piece to assemble backing.

3. Layer backing, batting, and quilt top. Baste. Quilt as marked or as desired.

4. From Fabric VI strips, make 9¼ yards of straight-grain binding. See page 22 for instructions on making and applying binding.

It's Okay to Be Different

This quilt goes to show that different can be splendid. A long-time favorite in appliqué, Sunbonnet Sue now makes her pieced debut. Scrap fabrics make sunbonnet fashions as cute as ever. What else is different? Look for one little girl going against the crowd.

Finished Size
Quilt: 59" x 93¾"
Blocks: 20 blocks, 10" x 12¼"

Quick-Piecing Techniques
Diagonal Corners (see page 12)
Diagonal Ends (see page 13)

Materials

	Fabric I (yellow solid)	3⅛ yards
	Fabric II (peach solid)	¼ yard
	Fabric III (purple solid or pindot)	¾ yard
	Fabric IV (turquoise print)	2½ yards
	Fabric V (assorted purple and pink prints)	scraps
	Fabric VI (green prints)	scraps
	Fabric VII (green solid)	⅛ yard
	Fabric VIII (red solid)	⅛ yard
	108"-wide backing fabric	2 yards
	Precut batting	81" x 96"
	½"-wide flat lace trim	2½ yards
	Pink and violet ⅜"-wide satin ribbon	2¼ yards each
	Pink and violet ½"-wide rickrack	2 yards each
	Green ribbon and rickrack	¼ yard each

Cutting

Cut all strips crossgrain, from selvage to selvage. For best use of yardage, cut pieces in order listed. Refer to diagrams to identify pieces.

From Fabric I (yellow solid), cut:

✱ Two 6½"-wide strips. From these, cut:
- Ten 6¼" x 6½". From these, cut 20 triangles (A6, B6) and 20 mirror-image triangles (A11, B11) as shown in Diagram 1. Store triangles in separate bags to avoid confusion.

✱ Two 5¼"-wide strips. From these, cut:
- Twenty 2½" x 5¼" (A1, B1).
- Twenty 1¾" x 5¼" (A5, B5).

✱ One 5"-wide strip. From this, cut:
- Eleven 2⅜" x 5". Cut 10 of these in half to get 19 (and one extra) of triangle A2 (Diagram 2). Cut one in half as shown to get one B2 triangle (and one extra).

✱ Six 3¼"-wide strips for sashing.

✱ Three 3"-wide strips. From these, cut:
- Twenty 3" squares (A15, B15).
- Twenty 2½" x 3" (A14, B14).
- Twenty 1¼" squares (A13a, B13a).

✱ Four 2"-wide strips for inner border.

✱ Twenty 1¾"-wide strips. From these, cut:
- Twenty 1¾" x 12¾" (A17, B17).
- Twenty 1¾" x 8" (A16, B16).
- Twenty 1¾" x 2¼" (A3, B3).
- Eighty 1¾" squares (A4a, A12, B4a, B12).
- Forty-six 1¾" x 4¼" for rick-rack borders.

From Fabric II (peach solid), cut:

✱ Two 2¼"-wide strips. From these, cut:
- Forty 1¾" x 2¼" (A9, B9).

From Fabric III (purple pindot), cut:

✱ Twelve 1¾"-wide strips. From these, cut:
- Ten 1¾" x 3½" (A13).
- Ninety-two 1¾" x 4¼" for rick-rack borders.
- Four 1¾" x 8" for border corners.

From Fabric IV (turquoise print), cut:

✱ Six 1¾"-wide strips. From these, cut:
- Forty-two 1¾" x 4¼" for rick-rack borders.
- Eight 1¾" x 8" for border corners.

✱ Eight 6"-wide strips for outer border.

✱ Eight 3"-wide strips for binding.

From Fabric V (purple and pink prints), cut:

Note: Cut pieces for nine pink blocks and 10 purple blocks.

✱ Six 6¼" x 6½" (three purple, three pink). Cut two each of triangles A6 and A11 from each piece (Diagram 1), enough for two blocks from each fabric. Cut a total of 20 purple triangles and 18 pink triangles. Discard extras.

✱ Nineteen 4¼" x 5¼" (A4).

✱ Nineteen 1¼" x 5½" (A7).

✱ Ten 2⅜" x 5" (five purple, five pink). Cut each piece in half as shown at left in Diagram 2 to get two A2 triangles for a total of 10 purple and nine pink triangles. Discard extra triangle.

✱ Nineteen 2¼" x 3" (A8).

✱ Nineteen 1¾" x 2¼" (A10).

From Fabric VI (green scraps), cut:

✱ One 6¼" x 6½". Cut as shown in Diagram 1 to get one each of triangles B6 and B11. Discard extra triangles.

✱ One 4¼" x 5¼" (B4).

✱ One 1¼" x 5½" (B7).

✱ One 1¾" x 2¼" (B10).

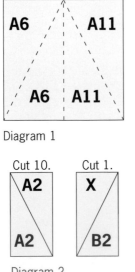

Diagram 1

Cut 10.   Cut 1.

Diagram 2

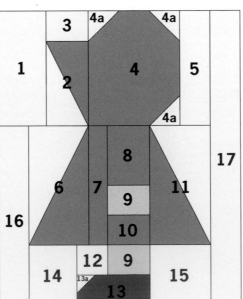

Block A—Make 19.

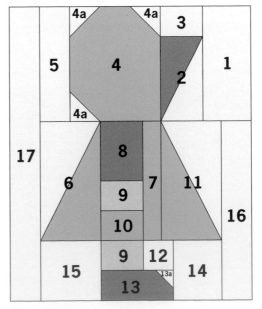

Block B—Make 1.

From Fabric VII (green solid), cut:

* One 1¾" x 3½" (B13).
* One 2¼" x 3" (B8).
* One 2⅜" x 5" (B2). Cut in half as shown in Diagram 2 to get one A2 triangle and one extra.

From Fabric VIII (red solid), cut:

* One 1¾"-wide strip. From this, cut:
  • Nine 1¾" x 3½" (A13).

Units for Block A

Refer to Block A Assembly Diagram throughout to identify units.

1. Use diagonal-corner technique to make one each of units 4 and 13.

2. For Unit 2, select one triangle each of fabrics I and V. Before you sew, trim 1" from the tip of each triangle (Diagram 3). Then join

triangles to make one of Unit 2 as shown. Press seam allowances toward Fabric V.

3. For units 6 and 11, trim 1" from triangle tips in same manner (Diagram 3). Then join triangles to make one of each unit.

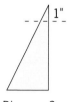

Diagram 3

Block A Assembly

Assemble this block in sections X, Y, and Z. Refer to Block A Assembly Diagram throughout to identify units and sections. Each completed block should measure approximately 10½" x 12¾".

Section X

1. Join units 2 and 3 as shown.
2. Join units 1, 2/3, 4, and 5 in a row as shown.

Section Y

1. Join units 8, 9, and 10 in a vertical row. Press seam allowances away from Unit 9.
2. Join units 6, 7, 8/9/10, and 11 in a horizontal row as shown.

Section Z

1. Join units 9 and 12 as shown.
2. Sew Unit 13 to bottom of combined unit 9/12.
3. Join units 14 and 15 to sides of combined unit.

Assembly

1. Join sections Y and Z as shown. Add Unit 16 to left side of combined sections.
2. Sew Section X to top of combined sections.
3. Join Unit 17 to right side of block.
4. Make nine of Block A with pink fabrics and 10 blocks with purple fabrics.
5. For each block, cut 4" of flat lace and 7" of rickrack. Tack rickrack in place ½" from skirt seam. Machine-stitch lace to edge of hat brim.

Block B Assembly

Block B is a mirror image of Block A. Make units in the same manner, but reverse angles of diagonal-corners. Referring to Block B Diagram, make one of Block B.

(continued)

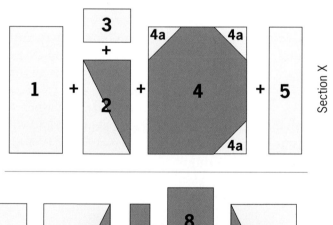

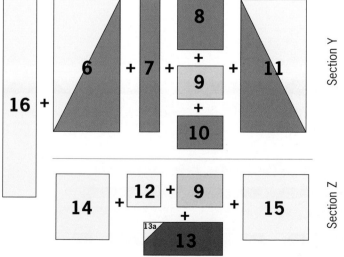

Block A Assembly Diagram

Row Assembly Diagram

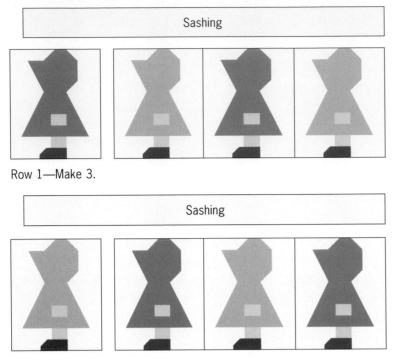

Sashing

Row 1—Make 3.

Sashing

Row 2—Make 2.

Quilt Assembly

Refer to photo and Row Assembly Diagram for placement of blocks in rows.

1. For each row, select two purple blocks and two pink blocks. Lay out row, alternating block colors as shown. Lay out three of Row 1, starting with a purple block, and two of Row 2, starting with a pink block. Position Block B as desired between any two purple blocks.

2. When satisfied with block placement, join blocks in each row.

3. Join a sashing strip to top edge of each row. Trim sashing even with row. Then join rows as shown in photo. Add last sashing strip to bottom of quilt.

Borders

1. Referring to instructions on page 17, measure quilt from top to bottom. Join two 2"-wide strips of Fabric I end-to-end to make a border for each quilt side. Measuring

out from center, trim borders to fit quilt length. Sew borders to quilt sides.

2. For first row of rickrack border, select forty-six 1¾" x 4¼" pieces of Fabric III and 46 matching pieces of Fabric I.

3. For top border, join nine Fabric III pieces and eight Fabric I pieces in a continuous diagonal end (Diagram 4). Start with a Fabric III piece and alternate fabrics as shown (Top and Bottom Border Diagram). With right sides facing, align Fabric I edge of border with top edge of quilt, matching centers, and sew. Trim border even with edge of quilt as necessary. Assemble and join bottom border to quilt in same manner.

4. Begin and end each side border with a 1¾" x 8" piece of Fabric III. Add 15 pieces of Fabric I and 14 pieces of Fabric III in a continuous diagonal end as shown (Side Borders Diagram). Make two side borders. Matching centers, stitch borders to quilt sides. Trim excess length at both ends as necessary.

5. Make next row of rickrack border in same manner. For top border, begin and end with a 1¾" x 8" piece of Fabric IV and add eight 1¾" x 4¼" pieces of Fabric III and seven pieces of Fabric IV, alternating fabrics as shown (Top and Bottom

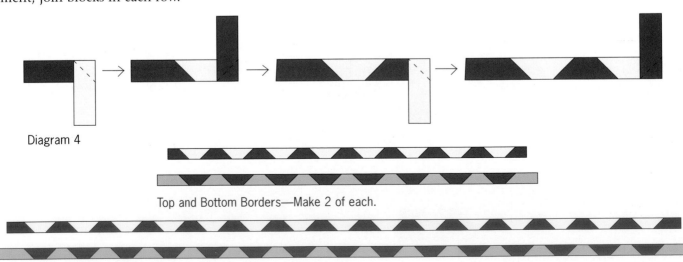

Diagram 4

Top and Bottom Borders—Make 2 of each.

Side Borders—Make 2 of each.

Borders Diagram). Make bottom border in same manner. Center borders on top and bottom edges of quilt, and stitch.

6. Begin and end each side border with an 8" piece of Fabric IV, adding 15 pieces of Fabric III and 14 pieces of Fabric IV as shown. Center borders on side edges of quilt and stitch.

7. From 6"-wide strips of Fabric IV, cut four 26"-long strips. Join two pieces each for top and bottom borders. Referring to instructions on page 17, measure quilt from side to side and trim borders to match quilt width. Sew borders to top and bottom edges of quilt.

8. For each side border, sew two 6"-wide strips to opposite ends of a leftover 16"-long strip. Measure quilt from top to bottom and trim borders to match quilt length. Sew borders to quilt sides. Press seam allowances toward outer borders.

Quilting and Finishing

1. Mark quilting design on quilt top as desired. On quilt shown, patchwork is outline-quilted and a row of 4"-high hearts is quilted in the border.

2. Layer backing, batting, and quilt top. Baste. Quilt as marked or as desired.

3. From Fabric IV strips, make 9 yards of straight-grain binding. See page 22 for instructions on making and applying binding.

4. For each block, cut 7" of ribbon. Tie each piece in a bow. Tack bow securely at bottom of hat brim.

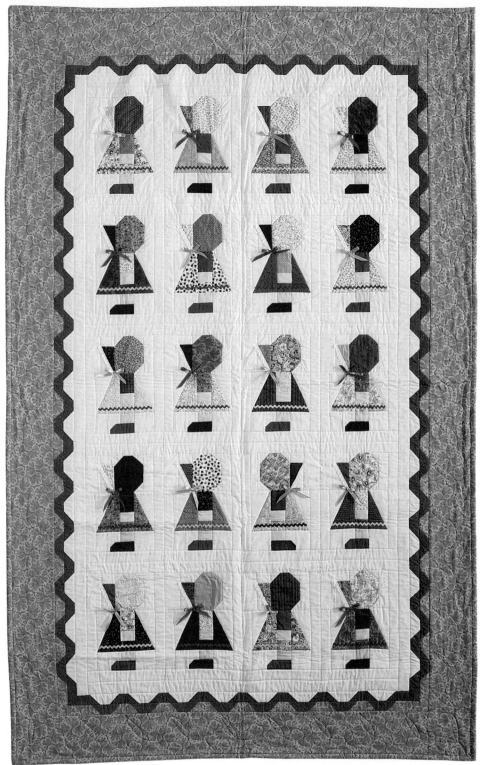

Primrose

Pretty in pink, this lovely bed of roses has the grace of appliqué, but it's pieced. Versatile quick-piecing techniques let us make lovely, traditional quilts like this with a speed that our grandmothers would envy.

Finished Size
Quilt: 88½" x 112"
Blocks: 12 primrose blocks, 16½" square
      36 rosebud blocks, 4½" square

Quick-Piecing Techniques
Strip Piecing (see page 12)
Diagonal Corners (see page 12)
Diagonal Ends (see page 13)

Materials

☐ Fabric I (white solid)	4⅞ yards
▨ Fabric II (pink print)	4⅛ yards
■ Fabric III (dark pink print)	2½ yards
☐ Fabric IV (yellow print)	1⅛ yards
▨ Fabric V (green solid)	1⅛ yards
108"-wide backing fabric	3½ yards
Precut batting	120" x 120"

Cutting

Cut all strips crossgrain, from selvage to selvage. For best use of yardage, cut pieces in order listed. Refer to diagrams to identify pieces.

From Fabric I (white solid), cut:

* Four 17"-wide strips. From these, cut:
  * Six 17" squares for setting squares.
  * Twenty-four 2¾" x 17" strips for sashing.
* Five 5"-wide strips. From these, cut:
  * Two 5" x 16⅞" (C4).
  * Two 5" x 10½" (C6).
  * Four 5" squares (C5).
  * Twenty-eight 4½" x 5" (C3).
* Eighteen 2"-wide strips. From these, cut:
  * Ninety-six 2" x 3½" (A1).
  * Four 2" x 12¼" (C9).
  * Four 2" x 12" (C10).
  * Twenty-eight 2" x 9" (C7).
  * Two 2" x 6½" (C8).

* Thirty 1¼"-wide strips. Set aside nine strips for Strip Set 1. From remaining strips, cut:
  * 696 1¼" squares (A2a, A3a, A5a, A9a, A16a, B3a, B5a, B9a, B16a).

From Fabric II (pink print), cut:

* Two 21½"-wide strips. From these, cut:
  * Three 18½" squares. Cut each square in quarters diagonally to get 10 C1 setting triangles and two extra.
  * Two 11" squares. Cut each square in half diagonally to get four C2 setting triangles.
  * Sixty-eight 2" squares (C7a, C8a, C9a, C10a).
* Twelve 3½"-wide strips for outer borders.
* Six 2¾"-wide strips. From these, cut:
  * Eighty-four 2" x 2¾" (A8, B8).
  * Forty-eight 1¼" x 2¾" (A17).

* Eleven 2"-wide strips. Set aside two strips for Strip Set 4. From remaining strips, cut:
  * Four 2" x 6" (C7c).
  * Four 2" x 4½" (C7b).
  * Ninety-six 2" x 3½" (A2).
* Sixteen 1¼"-wide strips. Set aside four strips for strip sets 2 and 3. From remaining strips, cut:
  * 132 1¼" x 2" (A6, A14, B6).
  * 192 1¼" squares (A10a).

From Fabric III (dark pink print), cut:

* Ten 3"-wide strips for binding.
* Nine 2¾"-wide strips. From these, cut:
  * Ninety-six 2¾" squares (A10).
  * Eighty-four 1¼" x 2¾" (A9, B9).
* Nineteen 1¼"-wide strips. Set aside four strips for strip sets 2 and 3. From remaining strips, cut:
  * Eighty-four 1¼" x 3½" (A5, B5).
  * 252 1¼" squares (A6a, A7, A8a, B6a, B7, B8a).

From Fabric IV (yellow print), cut:

* Thirty 1¼"-wide strips. Set aside six strips for strip sets 2, 3, and 4. From remaining strips, cut:
  * Twenty-four 1¼" x 17" (A19).
  * Twenty-four 1¼" x 15½" (A18).

From Fabric V (green solid), cut:

* Eight 2¾"-wide strips. From these, cut:
  * 168 2" x 2¾" (A3, A16, B3, B16).
* Nine 1¼"-wide strips for Strip Set 1.

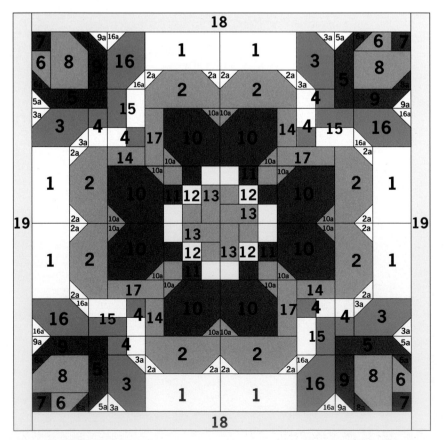

Block A—Make 12.

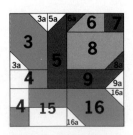

Block B—Make 36.

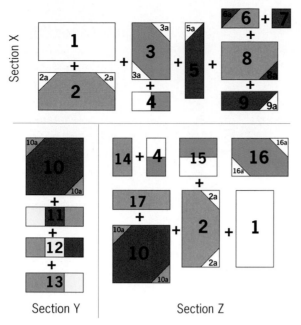

Quarter-Block Assembly Diagram

to Quarter-Block Assembly Diagram throughout. Each completed block should measure approximately 17" square.

Section X

1. Join units 1 and 2 as shown.
2. Join units 3 and 4 as shown.
3. Join units 6 and 7 as shown.
4. Sew unit 6/7 to top of Unit 8. Join Unit 9 to bottom of Unit 8.
5. Join units 1/2, 3/4, 5, and 6/7/8/9 in a horizontal row as shown.

Section Y

Join units 10, 11, 12, and 13 in a vertical row as shown.

Section Z

1. Join units 14, 4, 15, and 16 in a horizontal row as shown.
2. Sew Unit 10 to bottom of Unit 17.
3. Join units 10/17, 2, and 1 in a horizontal row as shown.
4. Join rows to complete section.

Assembly

1. Join Section Y to left side of Section Z.
2. Sew Section X to top of Y/Z to complete quarter-block.
3. Make four quarter-blocks for each block.
4. Referring to Block A Diagram, lay out four quarter-blocks in a square, placing rosebuds in corners. Join quarter-blocks in pairs; then join pairs.
5. Join Unit 18 to top and bottom edges of block. Then sew Unit 19 to sides to complete block.
6. Make 12 of Block A.

Units for Block A

Refer to Quarter-Block Assembly Diagram and strip-set diagrams to identify units. Store strip-set segments and assembled units in labelled zip-top bags.

1. For Strip Set 1, join 1¼"-wide strips of fabrics I and V as shown. Make nine strip sets. Press seam allowances toward Fabric V. From these strip sets, cut 168 1¼"-wide segments for Unit 4 and eighty-four 2"-wide segments for Unit 15.

2. For Strip Set 2, join 1¼"-wide strips of fabrics II, III, and IV as shown. Make two strip sets. Press seam allowances toward center strip. From these strip sets, cut forty-eight 1¼"-wide segments for Unit 11.

3. For Strip Set 3, join 1¼"-wide strips of fabrics II, III, and IV as

shown. Make two strip sets. Press seam allowances away from center strip. From these strip sets, cut forty-eight 1¼"-wide segments for Unit 12.

4. For Strip Set 4, join 1¼"-wide strip of Fabric IV and 2"-wide strip of Fabric II as shown. Make two strip sets. Press seam allowances toward Fabric II. From these strip sets, cut forty-eight 1¼"-wide segments for Unit 13.

5. Use diagonal-corner technique to make two each of units 2 and 10.

6. Use diagonal-corner technique to make one each of units 3, 5, 6, 8, 9, and 16.

Block A Assembly

Assemble this block in four quarter-block units. Make each quarter-block in sections X, Y, and Z. Refer

Block B Assembly

Referring to Block B Diagram, assemble units 3, 4, 5, 6, 7, 8, 9, 15, and 16 in same manner as for Block A. Make 36 of Block B for rosebud border.

(continued)

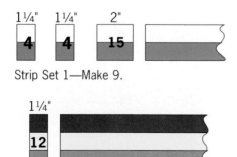

Strip Set 1—Make 9.

Strip Set 3—Make 2.

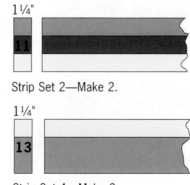

Strip Set 2—Make 2.

Strip Set 4—Make 2.

Row 1 — C2 · C1
Row 2 — C1
Row 3 — C2

C1

Setting Square · Setting Square

C1

C1

Setting Square · Setting Square

C1

C1

Setting Square · Setting Square

C1

C2 · C1

Row 4

Row 5 · C1

C1 · C2

Row 6

C1 · C1

Quilt Assembly Diagram

Quilt Assembly

Join blocks and setting squares in diagonal rows. Setting triangles C1 and C2, with sashing strips, fill in at sides and corners. Refer to Quilt Assembly Diagram throughout.

1. Referring to Sashing Diagram, join sashing strips to two sides of each C1 triangle and long edge of each C2 triangle. Trim ends of sashing even with triangle edges as shown.

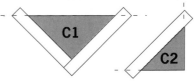

C1

C2

Sashing Diagram

2. For Row 1, join C2 unit to one side of Block A. Then sew two C1 units to opposite sides of block.

3. For Row 2, join two A blocks to opposite sides of one setting square. Press seam allowances toward square. Add C1 units to ends of row.

4. Join blocks, setting squares, and triangle units in diagonal rows. Complete rows 3–6 as shown.

5. Join rows in numerical order.

Borders

There are three borders on this quilt—a rosebud border, a scallop border, and an outer border of Fabric II. Refer to Border Diagrams throughout.

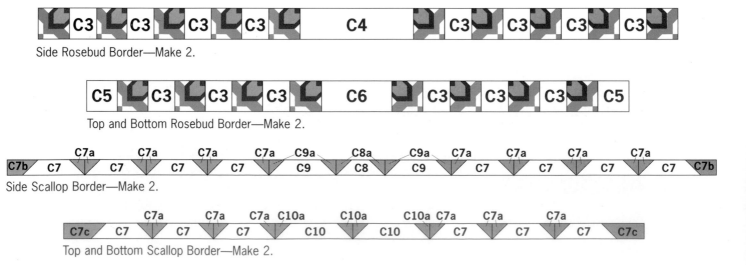

C3 · C3 · C3 · C3 · C4 · C3 · C3 · C3 · C3

Side Rosebud Border—Make 2.

C5 · C3 · C3 · C3 · C6 · C3 · C3 · C3 · C5

Top and Bottom Rosebud Border—Make 2.

C7b · C7 · C7a · C7 · C7a · C7 · C7a · C7 · C9a · C9 · C8a · C8 · C9a · C9 · C7a · C7 · C7a · C7 · C7a · C7 · C7a · C7 · C7b

Side Scallop Border—Make 2.

C7c · C7 · C7a · C7 · C7a · C7 · C7a · C10a · C10 · C10a · C10 · C10a · C7a · C7 · C7a · C7 · C7a · C7 · C7c

Top and Bottom Scallop Border—Make 2.

Rosebud Border

1. For side border, select 10 B blocks, eight C3, and one C4. Lay out units in a row, positioning rosebuds as shown. Join units in a row. Make two side borders.

2. Match center of border with center of quilt side. If border doesn't match quilt side at ends, adjust C4 seams as necessary. Sew borders to quilt sides.

3. For top border, select eight B blocks, six C3, two C5, and one C6. Join units in a row, positioning rosebuds as shown.

4. Match center of border with center of quilt's top edge. Adjust C6 seams as necessary to make ends match. Sew border to quilt.

5. Repeat steps 3 and 4 to make bottom border.

Scallop Border

1. Use diagonal-corner technique to make two of Unit C8 and four each of units C9 and C10 as shown.

2. Use diagonal-corner technique to make 20 of Unit C7 with two corners. Make eight more of Unit C7 with one corner.

3. Referring to diagram, join a C9 unit to each end of C8. Add three C7s to both ends of row; then add a one-corner C7 to row ends. To complete side border, use diagonal-end technique to add a C7b at each end of row. Note that these are mirror-image units. Make two side borders.

4. With right sides facing, pin side borders to quilt sides. Align C7 seams (between Fabric II corners) with centers of C3 units of rosebud borders. Sew borders to quilt sides.

5. Referring to diagram, join two C10 units. Add two C7s to both ends of row; then add a one-corner C7 to row ends. To complete border, use diagonal-end technique to add a C7c at each end of row. Make two borders. Pin and sew borders to top and bottom edges of quilt as you did for side borders.

Outer Border

1. For each border, join three 3½" strips of Fabric II end-to-end. Make four borders.

2. Referring to instructions on page 17, measure quilt from top to bottom. Measuring out from center, trim two border strips to match length. Sew borders to quilt sides.

3. Measure quilt from side to side. Trim remaining borders to match quilt width. Sew borders to top and bottom edges of quilt. Press seam allowances toward borders.

Quilting and Finishing

1. Mark quilting design on quilt top as desired. On quilt shown, patchwork is outline-quilted. If desired, make a stencil of Block A outline and mark block design in setting squares and rosebuds in C1 triangles and Fabric I border units.

2. Layer backing, batting, and quilt top. Baste. Quilt as marked or as desired.

3. From Fabric III strips, make 11⅝ yards of straight-grain binding. See page 22 for instructions on making and applying binding.

Grandmother's Violets

Grace and elegance bloom in this bed of pieced posies. In old-fashioned lavender or bright scrap fabrics, the medallion setting guarantees a bold effect. A scallop-like outer border sets this quilt apart from garden-variety patchwork.

Finished Size
Quilt: 81" x 109½"
Blocks: 26 violet blocks, 9" square
       48 leaf blocks, 9" square

Quick-Piecing Techniques
Strip Piecing (see page 12)
Diagonal Corners (see page 12)
Diagonal Ends (see page 13)
Four-Triangle Squares (see page 15)

Materials

☐	Fabric I (white-on-white print)	5¼ yards
▨	Fabric II (green print)	3 yards
▮	Fabric III (solid navy)	1⅛ yards
▮	Fabric IV (purple solid)	⅞ yard
▨	Fabric V (lavender solid)	2⅜ yards
☐	Fabric VI (yellow solid)	¼ yard
	Backing fabric	6½ yards
	Precut batting	120" x 120"

Cutting

Cut all strips crossgrain, from selvage to selvage. For best use of yardage, cut pieces in order listed. Refer to diagrams to identify pieces.

From Fabric I (white), cut:
* Three 9½"-wide strips. From these, cut:
  * Three 9½" squares (D).
  * Sixteen 5½" x 9½" (C3).
* Ten 5½"-wide strips. Set aside eight strips for strip sets 2 and 4. From remaining strips, cut:
  * Sixteen 4½" x 5½" (C2).
* Four 4½"-wide strips for Strip Set 3.
* Three 4¼"-wide strips. From these, cut:
  * Fifty-two 2" x 4¼" (A2).

* Four 4"-wide strips for Strip Set 3.
* Nine 3"-wide strips. Set aside six strips for Strip Set 4. From remaining strips, cut:
  * Thirty-two 3" squares (C1a).
* Three 1½"-wide strips for Strip Set 1.
* Eight 1¼"-wide strips. From these, cut:
  * 260 1¼" squares (A1a, A3a, A8b, A10b, A11a).
* From scraps, cut:
  * Fifty-two 1¾" squares (A11b).
  * Twenty-six 1" x 3½" (A9).

From Fabric II (green), cut:
* One 34" square for bias binding.
* Two 4½"-wide strips. From these, cut:
  * Sixteen 4½" squares (C1).

* Three 3¼"-wide strips. From this and scraps from previous steps, cut:
  * Fifty-two 2⅜" x 3¼" (A11).
* Twenty-one 2"-wide strips. Set aside 16 strips for strip sets 3, 4, 5, and 6. From remaining strips, cut:
  * Two 2" x 8" (E5).
  * Sixteen 2" x 6½" (E4).
  * Twenty-six 2" squares (A1).
* Eight 1¼" strips. Set aside five strips for strip sets 1 and 2. From remaining strips and scraps, cut:
  * 104 1¼" squares (A3b, A10a).

(continued)

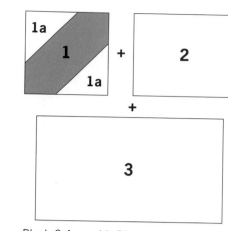

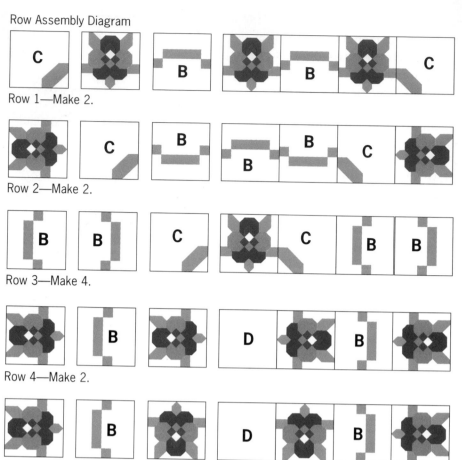

Row Assembly Diagram

Block C Assembly Diagram

Row 1—Make 2.

Row 2—Make 2.

Row 3—Make 4.

Row 4—Make 2.

Row 5—Make 1.

Block C Assembly

1. Use diagonal-corner technique to make one of Unit 1.
2. Join units 1 and 2. Add Unit 3 to bottom of combined units.
3. Make 16 of Block C.

Quilt Assembly

Refer to photo and Row Assembly Diagram for placement of blocks.
1. Lay out blocks for one each of rows 1, 2, 3, and 4 as shown. Note direction of each block.
2. For next row, lay out another Row 3, turning A and C blocks upside-down.
3. When satisfied with placement, join blocks in rows 1, 2, 3, 4, and 3. Join rows to make half of quilt.
4. Repeat steps 1–3 to make second half of quilt. Lay out both halves, turning one half upside-down for bottom of quilt.
5. Between two halves, lay out remaining blocks as shown for Row 5. When satisfied with placement, join blocks in Row 5.
6. Sew assembled quilt halves to both sides of Row 5.

Borders

1. For inner border, join three 2"-wide Fabric III strips end-to-end for each side border. For top and bottom borders, join two strips each.

2. Referring to instructions on page 17, measure quilt from side to side. Measuring outward from center of strips, trim top and bottom borders to match quilt width. Matching centers, sew borders to top and bottom edges of quilt.
3. Measure quilt from top to bottom; then trim remaining borders to match quilt length. Sew borders to quilt sides. Press seam allowances toward border.

3½"

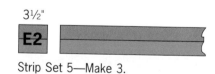

Strip Set 5—Make 3.

6½"

Strip Set 6—Make 3.

4. For middle border, repeat steps 1–3 with strips of Fabric V, eliminating top border (see photo).

Scallop Border

Refer to Border Assembly Diagram throughout.
1. For Strip Set 5, join 2"-wide strips of fabrics II and V as shown. Make three strip sets. From these, cut thirty-two 3½"-wide segments for Unit E2.
2. For Strip Set 6, join 3½"-wide strip of Fabric V and 2"-wide strip of Fabric II as shown. Make three strip sets. From these, cut fifteen 6½"-wide segments for Unit E3.
3. For bottom border, select two E1, eight E2, three E3, and four E4. Join units in a row as shown. Be sure top edge of row is even. Sew border to bottom edge of quilt.

4. For left side border, select 12 E2, six E3, and six E4. Join units in a row, keeping top of row even. Sew border to left side of quilt.

5. Sew E5 across E3/E1 scallop at bottom corner.

6. The right side border is a mirror image of the left. Join units as shown. Sew border to right side of quilt and complete bottom corner as before.

Quilting and Finishing

1. Mark quilting designs on quilt top as desired. On quilt shown, patchwork is outline-quilted. Use purchased stencils to mark swags, shells, and feathered wreaths in open areas.

2. Divide backing fabric into two 3¼-yard lengths. Cut one piece in half lengthwise. Join one narrow panel to each side of wide piece to assemble backing.

3. Layer backing, batting, and quilt top. Baste. Quilt as marked or as desired.

4. For bias binding, cut 34" square of Fabric II in half diagonally. Measuring from cut edges, cut 2"-wide diagonal strips. Join strips to make one strip 13 yards long.

5. See page 22 for directions on pressing and applying binding. Take special care to miter corners of scalloped border.

Border Assembly Diagram

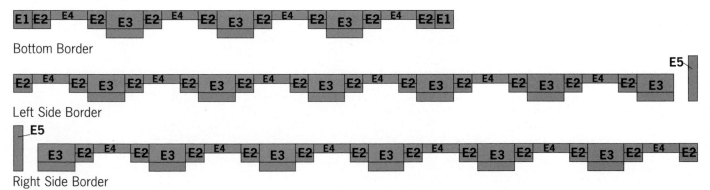

Keep On Truckin'

Complete with highways and road signs, this quilt has 15 pickups and panel trucks for aspiring little drivers to dream about. Scrap fabrics and two quick-piecing techniques make it easy to put together.

Finished Size
Quilt: 62" x 91"
Blocks: 15 truck blocks, 11" x 14"
 20 yield sign blocks, 3½" x 6½"
 8 stop sign blocks, 3½" square

Quick-Piecing Techniques
Strip Piecing (see page 12)
Diagonal Corners (see page 12)

Materials

	Fabric I (black solid)	2½ yards
	Fabric II (white solid)	2 yards
	Fabric III (red solid)	½ yard
	Fabric IV (green solid)	⅜ yard
	Fabric V (yellow solid)	⅞ yard
	Fabric VI (blue solid)	2 yards
	Fabric VII (assorted red, purple, green, yellow, and black)	Scraps
	Backing fabric	5½ yards
	Precut batting	81" x 96"
	Black fine-point fabric marker	

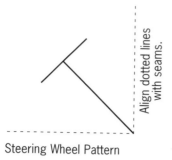

Align dotted lines with seams.

Steering Wheel Pattern

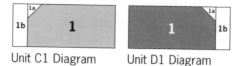

Unit C1 Diagram   Unit D1 Diagram

3. Assemble blocks as for blocks A and B. Make three of Block C and two of Block D.

Highway Sashing Assembly

1. Join 1½"-wide strips of fabric II and VI as shown (Strip Set 2 Diagram). Make six strip sets. From these, cut sixty-six 3½"-wide segments for sashing.

2. For horizontal sashing, join eight Fabric VI sashing squares and seven Strip Set 2 segments as shown (Sashing Diagram). Make six sashing strips.

3. For side borders, join 13 sashing squares and 12 segments of Strip Set 2 in same manner. Make two side borders.

4. Use a pin to mark center of each sashing strip and border.

Quilt Assembly

1. Referring to photo, sort truck blocks into five rows, with two pickups and one panel truck in each row. Trucks in each row should face same direction to avoid head-on collision!

2. When satisfied with placement, join blocks in each row.

3. Lay out rows as desired, placing a sashing strip between rows and at top and bottom as shown.

4. Match center of each sashing strip to center of adjacent row. Join rows and sashing. Trim ends of sashing to match block rows.

5. Matching centers, sew highway borders to quilt sides. Trim ends of borders to match top and bottom edges of quilt.

Road Sign Border Assembly

1. Use diagonal-corner technique to make 20 Block E yield signs (Block E Diagram) and eight Block F stop signs (Block F Diagram).

2. For top border, join eight Unit H, four of Block E, two Unit G (speed limit sign), and one Block F as shown (Border Diagram).

3. Join two 1½" x 25" strips of Fabric I. Matching center seam with center of Block F, sew strip to top edge of border. Repeat for bottom edge of border.

4. Repeat steps 2 and 3 to make bottom border.

5. Sew borders to top and bottom edges of quilt.

6. For each side border, select 14 Unit H, six Block E, four Unit G, and three Block F. Assemble borders in same manner (Border Diagram), alternating E blocks with G/H units. Cut four remaining H pieces down to 1½" x 3½" and sew these to two remaining F blocks. Sew F/H units to ends of row. Make two borders.

7. Join 1½" x 42" strips of Fabric I in pairs. Matching centers, sew strips to long edges of each border. Sew borders to quilt sides.

8. Sew Unit 18 to top and bottom of block.

9. Make six of Block A, using various fabric combinations.

10. Using a fine-tipped fabric pen, trace Steering Wheel Pattern onto Unit 4. For windshield, draw a line in the seam between units 4 and 5. (If you prefer, you can embroider windshield and steering wheel.)

Block B Assembly

Block B is a mirror image of Block A. Make units in the same manner. Referring to Block B Diagram, make four of Block B.

Blocks C and D Assembly

Blocks C and D are the same as blocks A and B, except for Unit 1. See Unit C1 Diagram and Unit D1 Diagram. Refer to Block Assembly Diagram throughout.

1. Use diagonal-corner technique to sew 1a to one corner of Unit 1. Add Unit 1b to side of unit.

2. Assemble remaining units as described for Block A.

3½"

Strip Set 2—Make 6.

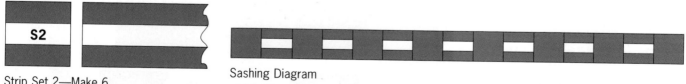

Sashing Diagram

Border Diagram

3. Pin borders to top edge, placing green square at left corner. Remove last red square on border if necessary. Sew border to top edge of quilt. Repeat for bottom border.

Outer Border

1. For each side border, join two 2½"-wide strips of Fabric VI to ends of one 10"-long strip. For top and bottom borders, join two 32"-long strips end-to-end.

2. Referring to instructions on page 17, measure quilt from top to bottom. Trim long borders to match length.

3. Measure quilt from side to side. Trim top and bottom borders to match quilt width.

4. Sew longer borders to quilt sides. Press seam allowances toward borders.

5. Sew Fabric I border corners to ends of remaining borders. Press seam allowances away from corners.

6. Sew pieced borders to top and bottom edges of quilt.

Quilting and Finishing

1. Mark quilting design on quilt top as desired. On quilt shown, patchwork is outline-quilted.

2. Divide backing into two 2¾-yard lengths. Cut one piece in half lengthwise. Join one narrow panel to each side of wide piece to assemble backing.

3. Layer backing, batting, and quilt top. Baste. Quilt as marked or as desired.

4. From Fabric I strips, make 9 yards of straight-grain binding. See page 22 for instructions on making and applying binding.

Traffic Light Border Assembly

1. For Strip Set 3, join 2½"-wide strips of fabrics III, IV, and V as shown (Strip Set 3 Diagram). Make two strip sets. From these, cut twenty 2½"-wide segments.

2. Referring to photo, join 10 segments end-to-end, sewing red to green. Make two borders.

2½"

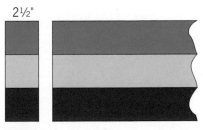

Strip Set 3—Make 2.

Sunflowers

A sawtooth border puts the finishing touch on a quilt that celebrates the warmth and joy of summer. Strip piecing and diagonal corners help make quick work of block construction. Sashing pulls it all together for a quilt that's a pleasure to make and own.

Finished Size

Quilt: 74" x 94"
Blocks: 24 flower blocks, 9" square
        12 flower and stem blocks, 9" x 19"

Quick-Piecing Techniques

Strip Piecing (see page 12)
Diagonal Corners (see page 12)
Triangle-Squares (see page 14)

Materials

	Fabric I (black solid)	3½ yards
	Fabric II (ivory print)	2⅝ yards
	Fabric III (light yellow print)	1 yard
	Fabric IV (gold print)	1 yard
	Fabric V (green print)	1⅝ yards
	Fabric VI (rust print)	2¾ yards
	Fabric VII (dark brown solid)	⅜ yard
	Backing fabric	5¾ yards
	Precut batting	81" x 96"

Cutting

Cut all strips crossgrain, from selvage to selvage. For best use of yardage, cut pieces in order listed. Refer to diagrams to identify pieces.

From Fabric I (black), cut:

* Eleven 3"-wide strips. Set aside nine strips for binding. From remaining strips, cut:
  * Eighty ⅞" x 3" (A5).

* Four 2¾"-wide strips for Strip Set 1.
* Eighteen 2½"-wide strips for borders.
* Ten 1½"-wide strips. Set aside four strips for Strip Set 2. From remaining strips, cut:
  * 160 1½" squares (A1a, A2a).
* Nine 1⅛"-wide strips. From these, cut:
  * 320 1⅛" squares (A6a, A7a).

From Fabric II (ivory print), cut:

* One 8¾"-wide strip. From this, cut:
  * One 8¾" x 12⅛" for E triangle-squares.
  * Two 4⅜" x 30" strips. From these, cut:
    * Twelve 4⅜" x 5" (C15).
* Three 2¾"-wide strips for Strip Set 3.   (continued)

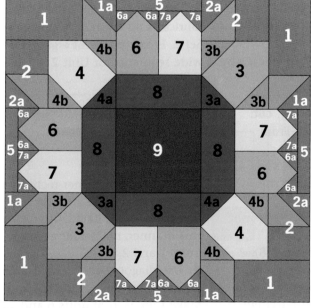

Block A—Make 20.

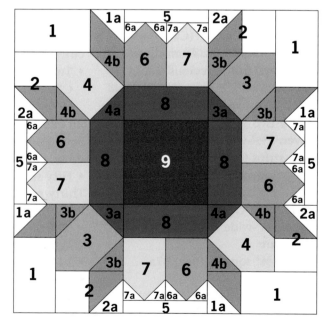

Block B—Make 4.

Block C Assembly

The flower of Block C is almost the same as Block B. Refer to Blocks A & B Assembly Diagram and Block C Assembly Diagram.

1. Assemble flower units as described for Block B. For one pair of units 6 and 7, include diagonal corners 6b and 7b (Block C Assembly Diagram). Replace one Unit 5 with a pieced unit, joining 5b to both sides of 5a as shown.

2. Use diagonal-corner technique to make two of Unit 11 for stem section.

3. Follow instructions for Block A to assemble sections X and Z. In Section Y, substitute units 5, 6, and 7 (Block C Assembly Diagram). Join flower sections as before.

4. For stem section, join units 10, 11, and 12 in a row as shown. Join units 13 and 14. Make another row of units 15, 11, and 16 as shown. Join rows to complete section.

5. Join flower to stem section to complete Block C.

6. Make 12 of Block C.

Quilt Assembly

Refer to Row Assembly Diagram for placement of blocks and sashing in vertical rows.

1. For Row 1, join nine sashing squares and eight sashing strips as shown. Make seven of Row 1. Press seam allowances toward sashing.

2. For Row 2, join four A blocks, two B Blocks, and one C block, sewing sashing strips between blocks as shown. Make two of Row 2.

3. For Row 3, join four A blocks and two C blocks with sashing strips between blocks as shown. Make two of Row 3.

4. For Row 4, join two A blocks and three C blocks with sashing strips between blocks as shown. Make two of Row 4.

5. Referring to photo, lay out rows 2, 3, 4, 4, 3, 2 side by side. Place a Row 1 between rows and at both sides. When satisfied with placement, join rows.

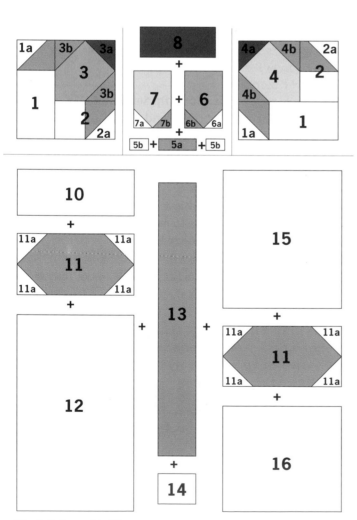

Block C Assembly Diagram

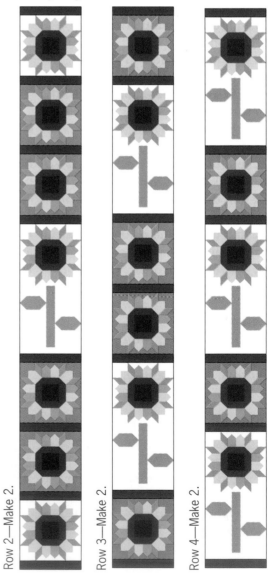

Row Assembly Diagram

Row 1—Make 7. Row 2—Make 2. Row 3—Make 2. Row 4—Make 2.

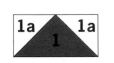

Block D—Make 56.

Sawtooth Border Diagram

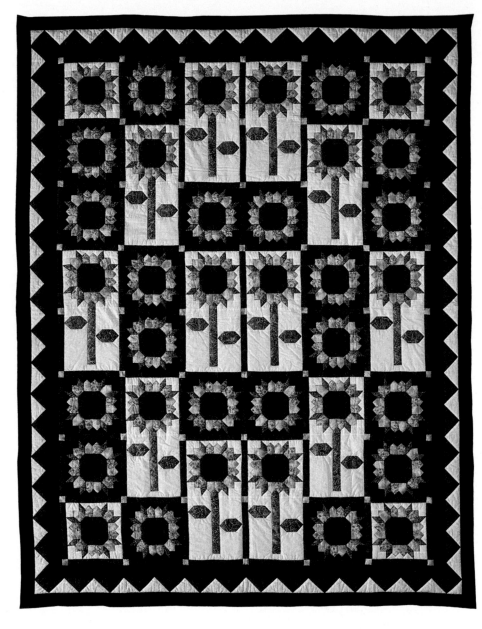

Borders

The inner and outer borders are plain strips of Fabric I. The middle border is a pieced sawtooth border.

Inner Border

1. For each border, join two 2½"-wide strips end-to-end.

2. Referring to instructions on page 17, measure quilt from top to bottom. Centering seam, trim two borders to match length. Sew borders to quilt sides.

3. Measure quilt from side to side. Trim remaining borders to match quilt width. Sew borders to top and bottom edges of quilt. Press seam allowances toward borders.

Sawtooth Border

1. Use diagonal-corner technique to make 56 of Block D.

2. Referring to triangle-square instructions on page 14, draw a 2 x 3-square grid of 3⅜" squares on wrong side of 8¾" x 12⅛" piece of Fabric II. Pair marked fabric with matching piece of Fabric VI, with right sides facing. Stitch grid as directed on page 14. Cut and press 12 triangle-squares.

3. For each side border, join 16 D blocks end-to-end (Sawtooth Border Diagram). Referring to photo, add an E block to both ends of each border. Sew borders to quilt sides. Press seam allowances toward inner border.

4. For top border, join 12 D blocks end-to-end. Add two E blocks to ends of row, checking photo to position Es correctly. Sew border to top edge of quilt. Repeat for bottom border.

Outer Border

1. For each side border, join three Fabric I strips end-to-end. For top and bottom borders, join two strips.

2. Repeat steps 2 and 3 for inner border to sew outer borders to quilt.

Quilting and Finishing

1. Mark quilting design on quilt top as desired. On quilt shown, patchwork is outline-quilted.

2. Divide backing into two 2⅞-yard lengths. Cut one piece in half lengthwise. Join one narrow panel to each side of wide piece to assemble backing.

3. Layer backing, batting, and quilt top. Baste. Quilt as marked or as desired.

4. From Fabric I strips, make 9¾ yards of straight-grain binding. See page 22 for instructions on making and applying binding.

Tea for Two

Tea with a friend is twice as nice with this little tablecloth or wall hanging.
Choose fabrics to complement your china, and you'll set a pretty table. Quilt rows
of "steam" over the cups or use a fabric marker to draw the lines.

Finished Size

Tablecloth: 49½" x 51½"
Blocks: 3 teapot blocks, 11" square
6 teacup blocks, 11" square

Quick-Piecing Techniques

Diagonal Corners (see page 12)
Diagonal Ends (see page 13)

Materials

☐	Fabric I (white-on-white print)	1⅛ yards
▨	Fabric II (pink print)	1⅛ yards
▨	Fabric III (pink solid)	1 yard
▨	Fabric IV (blue print)	¼ yard
▨	Fabric V (blue solid)	½ yard
	Backing fabric	3 yards
	Precut lightweight batting (optional)	72" x 90"
	Embroidery floss	

Cutting

Cut all strips crossgrain, from selvage to selvage. For best use of yardage, cut pieces in order listed. Refer to diagrams to identify pieces.

From Fabric I (white), cut:

* Two 5½"-wide strips. From these, cut:
  • Six 5½" x 11½" (B1).
* One 4½"-wide strip. From this and scrap from previous step, cut:
  • Three 4½" x 11½" (A1).
  • Six 2½" x 4½" (A10a).
* One 3½"-wide strip. From this, cut:
  • Six 3½" squares (B2).

* Two 2½"-wide strips. From these, cut:
  • Nine 2½" squares (A2, A4a, A4b).
  • Thirty-nine 1½" x 2½" (A9, B3, B6, B9a).
* Five 1½"-wide strips. From these, cut:
  • Two 1½" x 35" for side sashing.
  • Nine 1½" x 11½" (A11, B10).
  • Twenty-one 1½" squares (A3a, A7a, B7).

From Fabric II (pink print), cut:

* One 2½"-wide strip. From this, cut:
  • Four 2½" x 7½" (A4, A10).
  • Four 2½" squares (A3, A4b).

* Five 5"-wide strips for outer border.
* One 3½"-wide strip. From this, cut:
  • Four 3½" x 5½" (B5).

* One 1½"-wide strip. From this and scrap, cut:
  • Two 1½" x 7½" (A6).
  • Fourteen 1½" x 2½" (A7, A8, B6a).
  • Six 1½" squares (A2a, B8).

From Fabric III (pink solid), cut:

* Five 3"-wide strips for binding.
* Four 2"-wide strips for middle border.
* Three 1½"-wide strips. From these, cut:
  • Four 1½" x 9½" (B9).
  • Four 1½" x 5½" (B4).
  • Eight 1½" x 2½" (B3a).
  • Ten 1½" squares (A1a, B5a).
  • Four 1" x 7½" (A5).

From Fabric IV (blue print), cut:

* One 3½"-wide strip. From this, cut:
  • Two 3½" x 5½" (B5).
  • Two 2½" x 7½" (A4, A10).
  • Two 2½" squares (A3, A4b).

(continued)

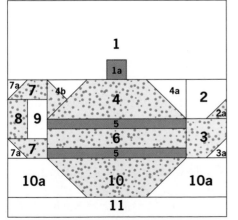

Block A—Make 2 with fabrics II/III.
Make 1 with fabrics IV/V.

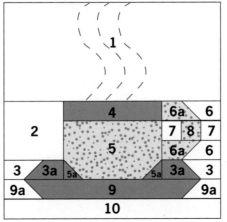

Block B—Make 4 with fabrics II/III.
Make 2 with fabrics IV/V.

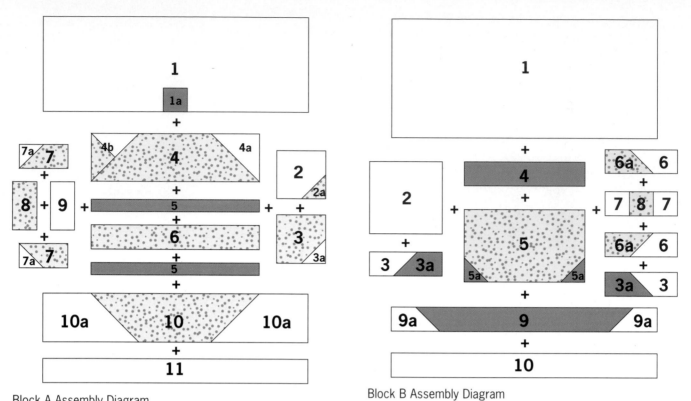

Block A Assembly Diagram

Block B Assembly Diagram

Units for Block B

Refer to Block B Assembly Diagram throughout to identify units.

1. Use diagonal-corner technique to make one Unit 5.

2. Use diagonal-end technique to make one of Unit 9 and two each of units 3 and 6 (note that second unit is a mirror image of the first, so be sure to angle diagonal ends appropriately).

Block B Assembly

Refer to Block B Assembly Diagram throughout.

1. Join units 2 and 3.

2. Join units 4 and 5 as shown. Sew 4/5 to right side of 2/3.

3. Sew Unit 7s to opposite sides of Unit 8.

4. Join units 6, 7/8, and 3 in a row as shown. Sew combined units to right side of 4/5.

5. Sew Unit 1 to top of block.

6. Join units 9 and 10 to bottom of block.

7. Make four of Block B with fabrics I, II, and III. Make two blocks with fabrics I, IV, and V.

✳ One 1½"-wide strip. From this, cut:
- One 1½" x 7½" (A6).
- Seven 1½" x 2½" (A7, A8, B6a).
- Three 1½" squares (A2a, B8).

From Fabric V (blue solid), cut:

✳ Four 2½"-wide strips for first border.

✳ Two 1½"-wide strips. From these, cut:
- Two 1½" x 9½" (B9).
- Two 1½" x 5½" (B4).
- Four 1½" x 2½" (B3a).
- Five 1½" squares (A1a, B5a).
- Two 1" x 7½" (A5).

Units for Block A

Refer to Block A Assembly Diagram throughout to identify units.

1. Use diagonal-corner technique to make two of Unit 7 and one each of units 2 and 3.

2. To make Unit 4b, draw a diagonal line on wrong side of 2½" square of Fabric I. Match marked square with 2½" square of Fabric II, with right sides facing. Stitch on

drawn line. Trim seam allowances to ¼" and press.

3. Use diagonal-corner technique to make one of Unit 4, using triangle-square for 4b.

4. Use diagonal-end technique to make one Unit 10.

5. Press under ¼" on three sides of square 1a. Matching raw edges, center square at bottom of Unit 1 and appliqué.

Block A Assembly

Refer to Block A Assembly Diagram throughout.

1. Join units 4, 5, and 6 in a row as shown.

2. Join units 2 and 3. Sew 2/3 to right side of 4/5/6 unit.

3. Join units 8 and 9. Add Unit 7s to top and bottom of 8/9 as shown. Sew 7/8/9 to left side of 4/5/6 unit.

4. Sew Unit 1 to top of block.

5. Sew units 10 and 11 to bottom of block.

6. Make two blocks with fabrics I, II, and III. Make one block with fabrics I, IV, and V.

Tablecloth Assembly

1. Referring to photo, arrange blocks in three horizontal rows with one teapot and two cups in each row.

2. When satisfied with block placement, join blocks in rows.

3. Join rows.

Borders

1. Join Fabric I sashing strips to sides of tablecloth.

2. Referring to instructions on page 17, measure quilt from side to side. Trim two Fabric VI border strips to match width. Sew borders to top and bottom edges of quilt.

3. Measure quilt from top to bottom; then trim remaining Fabric VI strips to match quilt length. Sew borders to quilt sides. Press seam allowances toward borders.

4. Sew Fabric III border strips to tablecloth in same manner.

5. For outer border, repeat Step 2 to sew Fabric II strips to top and bottom of tablecloth. For side borders, cut four 10"-long pieces from one remaining strip; then sew a short piece to each end of remaining two strips. Repeat Step 3 to sew side borders to tablecloth.

Quilting and Finishing

1. Mark quilting design on tablecloth as desired. Quilt shown is outline-quilted. Lightly draw wavy lines of steam over cups.

2. Divide backing into two 1½-yard lengths. Cut one panel in half lengthwise, discarding one half. Join remaining half panel to full piece to make backing with an off-center seam.

3. Layer backing, batting (if desired), and tablecloth. Quilt as marked or as desired. Use two strands of embroidery floss to quilt steam lines.

4. From reserved strips, make 5⅞ yards of binding. See page 22 for instructions on making and applying straight-grain binding.

Sweet Dreams

This quilt is the next best thing to sleeping under the stars. The sawtooth border encloses a galaxy of golden stars and smiling moons. Select a navy or black background fabric with white dots or tiny stars, and the heavens are at your fingertips.

Finished Size
Quilt: 82" x 102"
Blocks: 2 moon blocks, 18" x 22"
　　　　12 star blocks, 11" x 14"

Quick-Piecing Techniques
Diagonal Corners (see page 12)
Diagonal Ends (see page 13)
Triangle-Squares (see page 14)

Materials

■	Fabric I (navy dot)	4 yards
□	Fabric II (white with gold print)	1⅛ yards
■	Fabric III (gold print)	1¾ yards
□	Fabric IV (yellow solid)	¼ yard
■	Fabric V (grape print)	3 yards
	Fabric VI (green print)	¾ yard
	90"-wide backing fabric	3⅛ yards
	Precut batting	90" x 108"
	Embroidery floss	

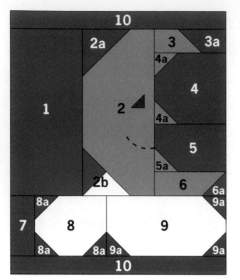

Block A—Make 1.

Cutting

Cut all strips crossgrain, from selvage to selvage. For best use of yardage, cut pieces in order listed. Refer to block diagrams to identify pieces.

From Fabric I (navy dot), cut:

✱ Four 14½"-wide strips. From these, cut:
  • Twelve 11½" x 14½" (D).
  • Two 6½" x 14½" (A1, B1).
  • One 7" square for triangle-square A2b, B2b.
  • Two 6½" squares (A4, B4).
✱ One 8"-wide strip. From this, cut:
  • One 8" x 19" for C6 triangle-squares.
  • Four 2" x 18½" (A10, B10).

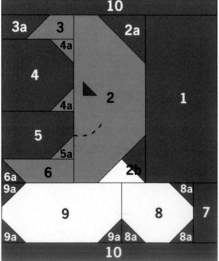

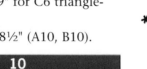

Block B—Make 1.

✱ Five 4½"-wide strips. From these, cut:
  • Four 4½" x 30" for sashing.
  • Two 4½" x 6½" (A5, B5).
  • Fourteen 4½" squares (A2a, B2a, C3).
✱ Four 4"-wide strips for inner border.
✱ Twelve 2½"-wide strips. From these, cut:
  • Thirty-six 2½" x 6½" (C1a, C11b).
  • Two 2½" x 5½" (A7, B7).
  • Fourteen 2½" x 4½" (A3a, B3a, C10).
  • Seventy-four 2½" squares (A6a, A8a, A9a, B6a, B8a, B9a, C2a, C7, C11a).

From Fabric II (white print), cut:

✱ One 8"-wide strip. From this, cut:
  • One 8" x 19" for C5 triangle-squares.
  • One 7" square for triangle-square A2b, B2b.
✱ Three 5½"-wide strips. From these, cut:
  • Two 5½" x 10½" (A9, B9).
  • Two 5½" x 6½" (A8, B8).
  • Twelve 4½" x 5½" (C2).
  • Twelve 2½" x 5½" (C11).
✱ One 4½"-wide strip. From this, cut:
  • Twelve 3½" x 4½" (C8).
✱ Four 2½"-wide strips. From these, cut:
  • Twelve 2½" x 6½" (C1).
  • Twenty-four 2½" x 3½" (C4).

From Fabric III (gold print), cut:

✱ One 8"-wide strip. From this, cut:
  • Two 8" x 19" for C5 and C6 triangle-squares.
✱ One 6½"-wide strip. From this, cut:
  • Two 6½" x 14½" (A2, B2).
  • Two 2½" x 6½" (A6, B6).
✱ Six 4½"-wide strips. From these and scraps, cut:
  • Twelve 4½" squares (C9).
  • Eighty 2½" x 4½" (A3, B3, E1).

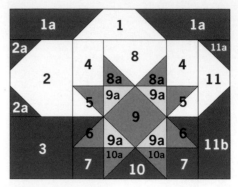

Block C—Make 12.

✱ Three 2½"-wide strips. From these and scraps, cut:
  • Fifty-four 2½" squares (A4a, A5a, B4a, B5a, C8a, C10a).

From Fabric IV (yellow solid), cut:

✱ Three 2½"-wide strips. From these, cut:
  • Forty-eight 2½" squares (C9a).

From Fabric V (grape print), cut:

✱ Nine 5½"-wide strips for outer border.
✱ Nine 3"-wide strips for binding.
✱ Ten 2½"-wide strips. From these, cut:
  • 160 2½" squares (E1a, saw-tooth border corners).
✱ From scraps, cut two moon eyes (see pattern, page 117).

From Fabric VI (green print), cut:

✱ Eight 2½"-wide strips for middle border.

Units for Block A

Refer to Block A Assembly Diagram throughout to identify units.

1. Use diagonal-corner technique to make one each of units 4, 5, 6, 8, and 9 as shown.

2. Sew diagonal corner 2a to Unit 2.

3. For Unit 2b, see page 14 for instructions on making triangle-squares. On wrong side of 7" square of Fabric II, draw one 4⅞" square. Draw one diagonal line from corner

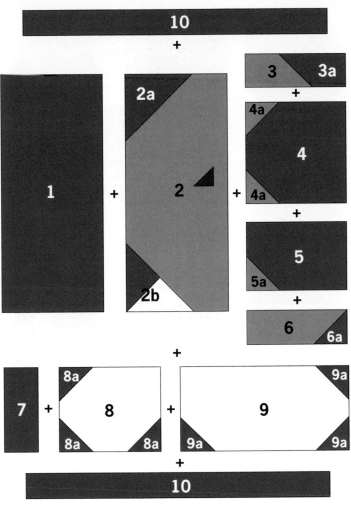

Block A Assembly Diagram

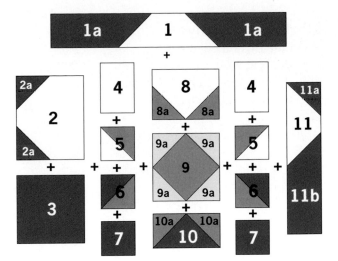

Block C Assembly Diagram

Units for Block C

Refer to Block C Assembly Diagram throughout to identify units.

1. See page 14 for instructions on triangle-squares. On wrong side of 8" x 19" Fabric II piece, draw a 2 x 6-square grid of $2\frac{7}{8}$" squares. With right sides facing, match marked fabric with 8" x 19" piece of Fabric III. Stitch grid as directed on page 14. Cut 24 triangle-squares from grid for Unit 5.

2. Using 8" x 19" pieces of fabrics I and III, repeat Step 1 to get 24 triangle-squares for Unit 6.

3. Use diagonal-corner technique to make one each of units 2, 8, 9, and 10.

4. Use diagonal-end technique to make one of Unit 1.

5. Use diagonal-corner and diagonal-end techniques to make one of Unit 11. *(continued)*

---

to corner. With right sides facing, match marked fabric square with 7" square of Fabric I. Stitch on both sides of diagonal line. Cut on all drawn lines to get two triangle-squares. Set aside one for Block B.

4. With right sides facing, position triangle-square at bottom corner of Unit 2. Use diagonal-corner technique to sew diagonal corner 2b as shown.

5. Use diagonal-end technique to make one of Unit 3.

4. Sew moon section to top edge of cloud section.

5. Sew a Unit 10 to top and bottom edges of block.

6. For eye, turn under ¼" on all raw edges. Position triangle on Unit 2 a little above the "nose" (Unit 4a) and 1" from seam. Appliqué eye in place.

7. Starting at 5a seam, lightly draw a curve on Unit 2 for smile. Use two strands of floss to backstitch smile.

Block A Assembly

Refer to Block A Assembly Diagram throughout.

1. Join units 3, 4, 5, and 6 in a vertical row as shown.

2. Join units 1, 2, and 3/4/5/6 in a row.

3. Join units 7, 8, and 9 as shown.

Block B Assembly

Block B is a mirror image of Block A. Make units in the same manner, but reverse angle of diagonal end and positions of diagonal corners. Referring to block diagram, make one Block B.

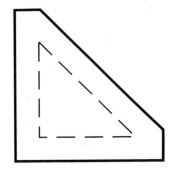

Eye Pattern

Block C Assembly

Assemble this block in vertical rows, adding Unit 1 to top of joined rows. Refer to Block C Assembly Diagram throughout.

1. Join units 2 and 3.

2. Join units 4, 5, 6, and 7 in a row as shown.

3. Join units 8, 9, and 10.

4. Join units 4, 5, 6, and 7 in a row as shown, making a mirror image of row in Step 2.

5. Join rows as shown. Add Unit 11 to right edge of block.

6. Sew Unit 1 to top of block.

7. Make 12 of Block C.

Quilt Assembly

Refer to Row Assembly Diagram for placement of blocks in rows. Assemble rows from top to bottom as shown. Press seam allowances toward D blocks throughout.

1. For sashing, join two 4½" x 30" strips of Fabric I end-to-end. Make two sashing strips.

2. For Row 1, join C blocks and Ds as shown. Sew sashing strip to left side of row; press seam allowances toward sashing and trim sashing even with blocks as necessary. Add Block A to top of row.

3. For rows 2 and 3, join C blocks and Ds as shown.

4. For Row 4, join C blocks and Ds as shown. Sew remaining sashing strip to right side of row; press seam allowances toward sashing and trim sashing even with blocks. Join Block B to bottom of row.

5. Join rows.

Borders

1. For inner border, join two 4"-wide Fabric I strips end-to-end. Aligning centers, sew border to top of quilt. Repeat for bottom border. Trim borders even with quilt sides.

2. For middle border, join two Fabric VI strips end-to-end for each border. Referring to instructions on

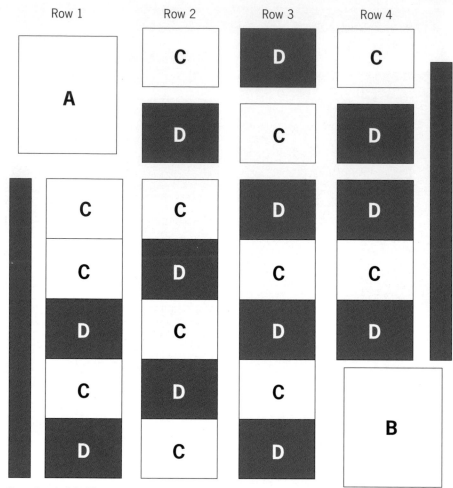

Row Assembly Diagram

page 17, measure quilt from top to bottom. Trim two borders to match length. Sew borders to quilt sides. Measure quilt width; then trim and sew remaining borders to top and bottom edges of quilt.

3. Use diagonal-corner technique to make 78 of Block E.

4. For each side sawtooth border, join 22 of Block E (Sawtooth Border Diagram). Referring to photo, sew borders to quilt sides, easing to fit as necessary.

Block E—Make 78.

5. For top sawtooth border, join 17 of Block E. Then join a 2½" square of Fabric V to each end of row. Join border to top edge of quilt, easing to fit as necessary. Repeat for bottom border.

6. Use 5½"-wide strips of Fabric V for outer border. Cut one strip in half.

7. For each side outer border, join a strip to both ends of one half-strip. Measure quilt from top to bottom; then trim borders to match quilt length. Sew borders to quilt sides.

8. Sew two remaining strips end-to-end. Measure quilt width; then trim and sew borders to top edge of quilt. Repeat for bottom border.

Sawtooth Border Diagram

Quilting and Finishing

1. Mark quilting design on quilt top as desired. Quilt shown is outline-quilted, with hand-drawn stars and clouds randomly quilted in D blocks and outer border.

2. Layer backing, batting, and quilt top. Baste. Quilt as desired.
3. From reserved strips, make 10½ yards of binding. See page 22 for instructions on making and applying straight-grain binding.

Field *of Flowers*

Combine appliqué with quick-piecing techniques to showcase your quiltmaking talents. Use scrap fabrics to piece the blossoms; then appliqué stems and leaves onto the assembled quilt. If you like, appliqué flowers on the fence and over the border. See page 125 for instructions on freezer-paper appliqué and how to make bias stems quickly and easily. Turn to page 126 for another version of this lovely garden.

Finished Size

Quilt: 80½" x 104¼"
Blocks: 30 flower blocks, 7½" square
      36 nine-patch blocks, 7½" square
      14 fence blocks, 2½" x 16¼"
      7 appliqué flowers

Quick-Piecing Techniques

Strip Piecing (see page 12)
Diagonal Corners (see page 12)

Materials

	Fabric I (mint green print)	6¼ yards
	Fabric II (dark green solid)	2⅜ yards
	Fabric III (white-on-white print)	⅞ yard
	Fabric IV (assorted yellows and golds)	Scraps
	Fabric V (assorted pastel prints)	Scraps
	Fabric VI (leaf green solid)	1¼ yards
	Backing fabric	6¼ yards
	Precut batting	90" x 108"
	Freezer paper for appliqué	

Cutting

Cut all strips crossgrain, from selvage to selvage. For best use of yardage, cut pieces in order listed. Refer to diagrams to identify pieces. Appliqué patterns are on page 130. See page 125 for tips on cutting appliqué pieces with freezer paper.

From Fabric I (mint green print), cut:

✳ Three 8"-wide strips. From these, cut:
  • Six 8" squares (spacer square).
  • Twelve 3" x 8" (E).

✳ Eleven 5½"-wide strips. Set aside five strips for Strip Set 3 and outer borders. From remaining strips, cut:
  • Six 5½" x 34" for outer borders.
  • Five 5½" x 8" (I).
  • One 3" x 5½" (D).

✳ One 4¼"-wide strip for Strip Set 3.

✳ Eighteen 3"-wide strips. Set aside 14 strips for strip sets 1, 2, and 3. From remaining strips, cut:
  • Four 3" x 13" (H).
  • Four 3" squares (F).
  • Thirty 1¾" x 3" (A8).
  • Thirty 1⅛" x 3" (A9).

✳ Eight 1¾"-wide strips. From these, cut:
  • Thirty 1¾" x 3⅝" (A6).
  • Sixty 1¾" x 2⅜" (A5).
  • Twenty-eight 1¾" squares (C1a).

✳ Twenty-six 1⅛"-wide strips. From these, cut:
  • Thirty 1⅛" x 3⅝" (A7).
  • 120 1⅛" x 2⅜" (A4).
  • 600 1⅛" squares (A1a, A2a).

✳ Nine 3"-wide strips for binding.

(continued)

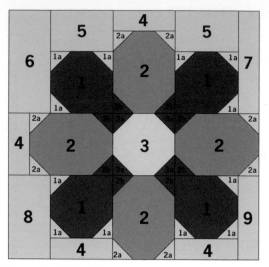

Block A—Make 30.

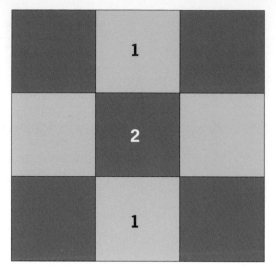

Block B—Make 36.

From Fabric II (dark green), cut:

* Eighteen 3"-wide strips. Set aside 17 strips for strip sets 1 and 2. From remaining strip, cut:
  * Seven 3" squares (G).
* Ten 2"-wide strips for inner border.

From Fabric III (white), cut:

* One 16¾"-wide strip. From this, cut:
  * Fourteen 3" x 16¾" (C1).
* Two 3"-wide strips for Strip Set 3.

From Fabric IV (assorted yellows), cut:

* Thirty 2⅜" squares (A3).
* Seven appliqué flower centers (Pattern 3).

From Fabric V (assorted pastels), cut:

* Four 2⅜" squares (A1) for each of 30 blocks.
* Four 2⅜" x 3" (A2) for each of 30 blocks.
* Twelve 1⅛" squares (A2b, A3a) for each of 30 blocks.
* Four of Pattern 1 for each of seven appliquéd flowers.
* Four of Pattern 2 for each of seven appliquéd flowers.

From Fabric VI (leaf green), cut:

* One 34" square for bias stems.
* Forty leaves for appliqué (Pattern 2).

Units for Block A

Refer to Block A Assembly Diagram throughout to identify units.

1. Use diagonal-corner technique to make four each of units 1 and 2.

2. Use diagonal-corner technique to make one of Unit 3.

Block A Assembly

Assemble this block in sections X, Y, and Z. Each completed section should measure approximately 8" wide. Refer to Block A Assembly Diagram throughout.

Section X

1. Sew Unit 5 to top edges of two Unit 1s. Be sure each Unit 1 is turned to position fabrics as shown.

2. Sew Unit 4 to top edge of Unit 2.

3. Join a 1/5 unit to sides of 2/4 unit.

4. Sew units 6 and 7 to sides of row.

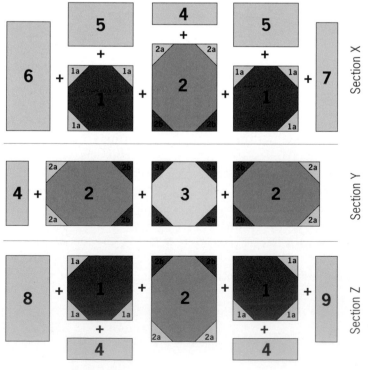

Block A Assembly Diagram

Section Y

Join units 2, 3, and 4 in a row as shown.

Section Z

1. Sew Unit 4 to bottom edges of two Unit 1s. Be sure each Unit 1 is turned to position fabrics as shown.
2. Join a 1/4 unit to sides of Unit 2.
3. Sew units 8 and 9 to sides of row.

Assembly

Join sections to assemble block. Make 30 blocks, using as many fabric combinations as desired.

Block B Assembly

Refer to strip set diagrams and Block B Assembly Diagram to identify units.
1. For Strip Set 1, join 3"-wide strips of fabrics I and II. Press seam allowances toward Fabric II. Make seven strip sets. From these, cut seventy-two 3"-wide segments for Unit 1. Cut another 17 units and set aside for quilt assembly.

2. For Strip Set 2, join 3"-wide strips of fabrics I and II as shown. Press seam allowances toward Fabric II. Make three strip sets. From these, cut thirty-six 3"-wide segments for Unit 2. Cut another four units and set aside for quilt assembly.
3. To assemble block, join two Unit 1s and one Unit 2 as shown.
4. Make 36 of Block B.

(continued)

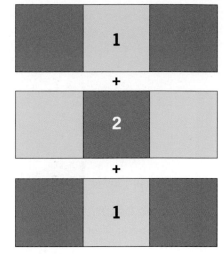

Block B Assembly Diagram

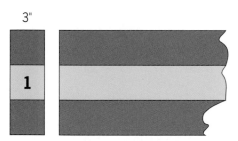

Strip Set 1—Make 7.

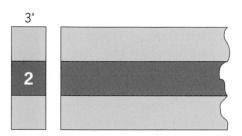

Strip Set 2—Make 3.

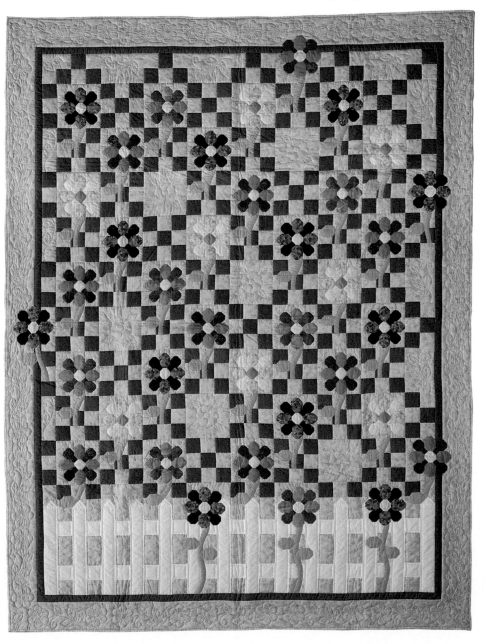

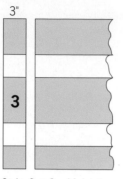

3"

3

Strip Set 3—Make 1.

Fence Row Assembly

1. Use diagonal-corner technique to make 14 of Block C.

2. For Strip Set 3, join 3"-wide strips of Fabric III and 4¼"-wide strip, 5½"-wide strip, and 3"-wide strip of Fabric I as shown (Strip Set 3 Diagram). Press seam allowances toward Fabric I. From this strip set, cut thirteen 3"-wide segments.

3. Join C blocks and strip-set segments in a row, alternating blocks and segments as shown for Fence Row (Row Assembly Diagram).

Row Assembly

Refer to photo and Row Assembly Diagram for placement of blocks and sashing units in rows.

1. For Sashing Row 1, join one D, five G, and four H as shown to make one row. Press seam allowances toward G squares.

2. For Sashing Row 2, join four Strip Set 1 segments, four E, two F, and one G as shown. Press seam allowances toward Fabric II. Make two of Sashing Row 2. Sew one row to bottom of Sashing Row 1. Sew second row to top of Fence Row.

3. Select four A blocks and four B blocks for each block row. Following Row Assembly Diagram, arrange blocks on the floor, moving blocks around to find a nice balance of scrap fabrics and color. Sprinkle in the six spacer squares in place of some A blocks, referring to photo. Alternate five of Block Row 1 and four of Block Row 2, adding sashing pieces and strip-set segments to row ends as shown.

4. When satisfied with arrangement of blocks, join blocks and sashing pieces in each row.

5. Lay out joined rows (including Fence Row) on floor to recheck position of blocks and sashing pieces. Do not join rows yet—there's some appliqué to do first!

Appliqué

1. Cut 34" square of Fabric VI in half diagonally. Starting from cut edges, cut 1¾"-wide diagonal strips (Diagram 1). From these, cut thirty 7½"-long strips, three 15"-long strips, and four 4"-long strips.

1¾"

Diagram 1

2. With wrong sides facing and edges aligned, fold each bias strip in half lengthwise. Machine-stitch ¼" from raw edge, making a narrow tube. On ironing board, flatten tube, rolling seam allowance to center. Press tube, pressing seam allowances open (Diagram 2).

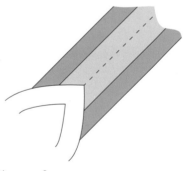

Diagram 2

3. Pin a 4"-long stem to each A block in last block row, centering end of stem over Unit 2 at bottom edge of flower and matching right sides and raw edges.

4. Pin 7½"-long stems to bottom of remaining A blocks in same manner. Set aside seven stems for appliquéd flowers.

5. Sew block rows together, securing stem ends in seams. Gently twist each stem into a gentle curve and pin in place on B blocks.

Row Assembly Diagram

| D | G | H | G | H | G | H | G | H | G |

Sashing Row 1—Make 1.

| F | 1 | E | 1 | E | 1 | E | 1 | E | G F |

Sashing Row 2—Make 2.

Block Row 1—Make 5.

Block Row 2—Make 4.

Fence Row—Make 1.

Freezer-Paper Appliqué

Freezer paper makes appliqué so easy, you may wonder what you did without it. Freezer paper lets you turn the edges of each piece smoothly without a lot of fuss.

1. Trace pattern onto uncoated (dull) side of a piece of freezer paper. Cut a template for each appliqué piece. For example, this quilt has 37 leaves, so you'll need 37 freezer-paper templates of Pattern 2.

2. Position template on wrong side of appliqué fabric, with coated side against fabric. Using a warm iron, press for about five seconds until the coating melts just enough for the paper to stick to the fabric.

3. Using the paper edge as a guide, cut out the appliqué shape, adding a ¼" seam allowance around the template (Photo A).

4. Press seam allowances over edge of template (Photo B). If desired, use glue stick to put a bit of glue around template edges to hold seam allowances in place.

5. Pin appliqués in place on quilt. Hand-sew pieces in place with a blindstitch. If you prefer, use your sewing machine's blindhem stitch and nylon ("invisible") thread.

6. When appliqué is complete, trim background fabric under appliqué and remove freezer paper (Photo C).

7. Press appliqué facedown on a towel. Use a light spray of water if desired.

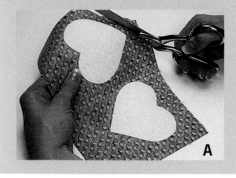

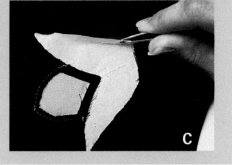

6. Following instructions for freezer-paper appliqué, prepare 30 leaves. Pin a leaf in place adjacent to each stem. Appliqué stems and leaves.

7. Finish bottom of each stem one of two ways, as desired. You can turn under end of stem and appliqué in place. Or use a seam ripper to open seam in center of Block B so you can insert end of stem; then machine-stitch opening closed through all layers. Trim stem to seam allowance.

8. Prepare appliqué pieces for three flowers. Position flowers on fence as shown. Pin or glue back petals first (Pattern 1); then front petals (Pattern 2) and center (Pattern 3) last. Pin end of 15"-long stem under each flower. Curve stem, aligning bottom of stem with bottom of Fence Row. Position leaves as shown. Appliqué flowers, stems, and leaves on Fence Row.

Borders

1. For inner border, join three 2"-wide strips of Fabric II end-to-end for each side border. Join two strips for top and bottom borders.

2. Referring to instructions on page 17, measure quilt from top to bottom. Trim side borders to match length. Matching centers, sew borders to quilt sides.

3. Measure quilt from side to side; then trim remaining borders to match quilt width. Sew borders to top and bottom edges of quilt.

4. For outer border, join three 5½" x 34" strips of Fabric I end-to-end for side borders. Join two full-length strips end-to-end for top and bottom borders. Repeat steps 2 and 3 to sew borders to quilt.

5. Prepare appliqué pieces for four flowers. Referring to photo, position flowers, stems, and leaves on border (two on right border, one at top, one on left border). Appliqué.

Quilting and Finishing

1. Mark quilting design on quilt top as desired. On quilt shown, patchwork is outline-quilted. Border vine is a purchased stencil—look for a similar stencil at your local quilt shop.

2. Divide backing into two 3⅛-yard lengths. Cut one piece in half lengthwise. Join one narrow panel to each side of wide piece to assemble backing.

3. Layer backing, batting, and quilt top. Baste. Quilt as marked or as desired.

4. From Fabric I strips, make 10½ yards of straight-grain binding. See page 22 for instructions on making and applying binding.

Field of Flowers Wall Hanging

A white picket fence against a blue sky calls out for pretty pastel flowers.
Scaled down from the full-size quilt on page 120, this wall hanging
suggests another color scheme for a quick-pieced meadow.

Finished Size

Quilt: 55" x 61"
Blocks: 7 flower blocks, 7½" square
10 nine-patch blocks, 7½" square
9 fence blocks, 2½" x 16¼"
3 appliqué flowers

Quick-Piecing Techniques

Strip Piecing (see page 12)
Diagonal Corners (see page 12)
Diagonal Ends (see page 13)

Materials

	Fabric I (medium blue print)	3 yards
	Fabric II (dark blue print)	¾ yard
	Fabric III (white-on-white print)	¾ yard
	Fabric IV (assorted pastel prints)	Scraps
	Fabric V (green print)	⅝ yard
	Backing fabric	3⅝ yards
	Precut batting	72" x 90"

Cutting

Cut all strips crossgrain, from selvage to selvage, except as noted. For best use of yardage, cut pieces in order listed. Refer to block diagrams to identify pieces. Appliqué patterns are on page 130.

From Fabric I (medium blue), cut:

✱ One 5½"-wide strip for Strip Set 3.
✱ One 4¼"-wide strip for Strip Set 3.
✱ Six 3"-wide strips for strip sets 1, 2, and 3.
✱ One 8" x 65" lengthwise strip. From this, cut:
  • Three 8" squares (spacer square).
  • Two 5½" x 8" (D).
  • Three 3" x 8" (E).

✱ Two 5½" x 48" lengthwise strips and two 5½" x 65" strips for outer border.
✱ Four 3" x 65" lengthwise strips for binding.
✱ Three 1¾"-wide strips. From these, cut:
  • Seven 1¾" x 3⅝" (A6).
  • Seven 1¾" x 3" (A8).
  • Fourteen 1¾" x 2⅜" (A5).
  • Eighteen 1¾" squares (C1a).
✱ One 1⅛"-wide strip. From this and scraps, cut:
  • Seven 1⅛" x 3⅝" (A7).
  • Seven 1⅛" x 3" (A9).
  • Twenty-eight 1⅛" x 2⅜" (A4).
  • 140 1⅛" squares (A1a, A2a).

From Fabric II (dark blue), cut:

✱ Five 3"-wide strips for strips sets 1 and 2.
✱ Five 1¾"-wide strips for inner border.

From Fabric III (white), cut:

✱ One 16¾"-wide strip. From this, cut:
  • Nine 3" x 16¾" (C1).
✱ Two 3"-wide strips for Strip Set 3.

(continued)

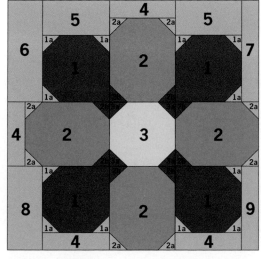

Block A—Make 7.

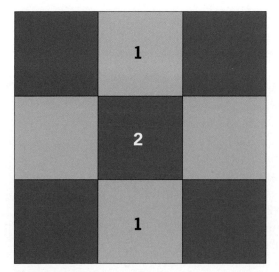

Block B—Make 10.

From Fabric IV (assorted pastels), cut:

✱ Five 2⅜" squares (A1, A3) for each of seven blocks.

✱ Four 2⅜" x 3" (A2) for each of seven blocks.

✱ Twelve 1⅛" squares (A2b, A3a) for each of seven blocks.

✱ Four of Pattern 1 for each of three appliqué flowers.

✱ Four of Pattern 2 for each of three appliqué flowers.

✱ One of Pattern 3 for each of three appliqué flowers.

From Fabric V (green), cut:

✱ One 18" square for bias stems.

✱ Eleven leaves for appliqué (Pattern 2).

Block A Assembly

Refer to Block A Assembly Diagram throughout to identify units.

1. Use diagonal-corner technique to make four each of units 1 and 2.

2. Use diagonal-corner technique to make one of Unit 3.

3. Follow instructions for Block A Assembly on page 122. Make seven of Block A.

Block B Assembly

Refer to strip set diagrams and Block B Assembly Diagram to identify units.

1. For Strip Set 1, join 3"-wide strips of fabrics I and II as shown. Make two strip sets. Press seam allowances toward Fabric II. From these, cut twenty-four 3"-wide segments for Unit 1. Set aside four segments for quilt assembly.

2. For Strip Set 2, join 3"-wide strips of fabrics I and II as shown. Press seam allowances toward Fabric II. From this strip set, cut thirteen 3"-wide segments. Set aside three segments for quilt assembly.

3. To assemble block, join two Units 1s and one Unit 2 as shown.

4. Make 10 of Block B.

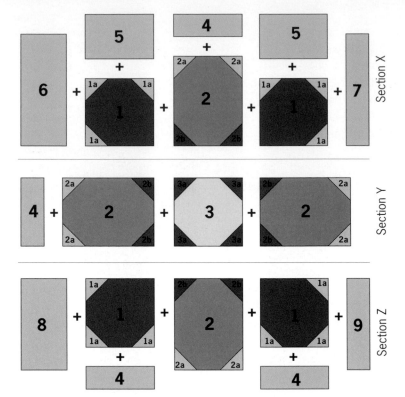

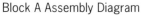

Block A Assembly Diagram

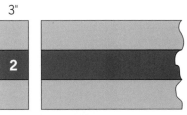

Strip Set 1—Make 2.

Strip Set 2—Make 1.

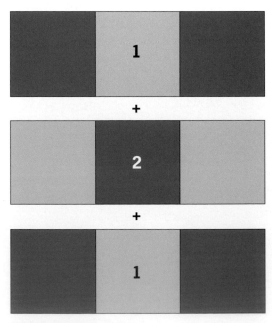

Block B Assembly Diagram

Fence Row Assembly

1. Use diagonal-corner technique to make nine of Block C (Block C Diagram).

2. For Strip Set 3, join 3"-wide strips of Fabric III and 4¼"-wide, 5½"-wide strip, and 3"-wide strip of Fabric I as shown. Press seam allowances toward Fabric I. From this strip set, cut eight 3"-wide segments for Fence Row.

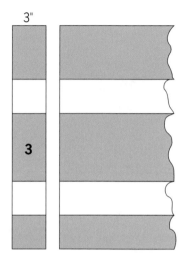

Strip Set 3—Make 1.

3. Join C blocks and strip-set segments in a row, alternating blocks and segments as shown (Row Assembly Diagram).

Row Assembly

Refer to photo and Row Assembly Diagram for placement of blocks and sashing units in rows.

1. Select blocks, spacer squares, and strip-set segments for each row as shown. Arrange blocks on the floor, moving blocks around to find a nice balance of scrap fabrics and color. Sprinkle in the three spacer squares in place of A blocks in some rows. Lay out two of Row 1 and two of Row 2 as shown, alternating rows.

2. When satisfied with arrangement of blocks, join blocks and sashing pieces in each row. Lay out rows on floor to recheck position of blocks and sashing pieces. Do not join rows yet; wait until appliqué is done.

3. For Row 3, join three E strips and two Strip Set 1 segments as shown. Remove one Fabric I square from remaining Strip Set 2 segment; then sew segment to end of row as shown.

4. Sew Row 3 to top of Fence Row.

Appliqué

1. Cut 18" square of Fabric VI in half diagonally. Starting from cut edges, cut 1¾"-wide diagonal strips (see Diagram 1, page 124). From these strips, cut six 7½"-long strips, two 4"-long strips, and two 15"-long strips for stems.

2. Follow steps 2–9 on page 124 to prepare and appliqué stems and leaves for pieced blocks.

3. Prepare appliqué pieces for two flowers. Position flowers on fence as shown. Curve 15"-long stem from bottom of flower to bottom of Fence Row. Position leaves as shown. Appliqué stem, leaves, and flowers on Fence Row.

Borders

1. Referring to instructions on page 17, measure quilt from side to side. Trim two 1¾"-wide strips of Fabric II to match quilt width. Sew borders to top and bottom edges of quilt.

2. Cut one remaining Fabric II strip into four 10" pieces. Sew one piece onto each end of remaining border strips to make side borders.

3. Measure quilt from top to bottom; then trim side borders to match quilt length. Matching centers, sew borders to quilt sides.

4. For outer border, repeat steps 1 and 3 to sew 5½"-wide strips of Fabric I to quilt.

5. Prepare appliqué pieces for remaining flower. Referring to photo, place flower and stem on right border. Appliqué. *(continued)*

Row Assembly Diagram

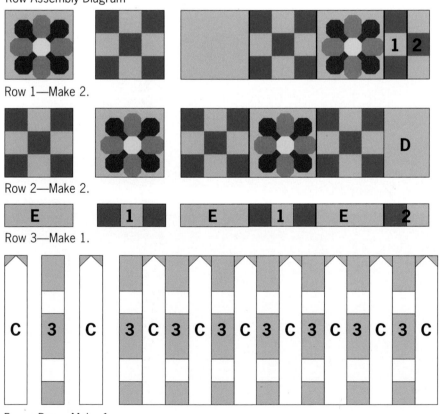

Row 1—Make 2.

Row 2—Make 2.

Row 3—Make 1.

Fence Row—Make 1.

Quilting and Finishing

1. Mark quilting design on quilt top as desired. On quilt shown, patchwork is outline-quilted. The cable quilted in border is a purchased stencil. Look for a similar one at your local quilt shop.

2. Divide backing into two equal lengths. Cut one piece in half lengthwise. Discard one narrow panel. Join remaining narrow panel to one side of wide piece to assemble backing with off-center seam.

3. Layer backing, batting, and quilt top. Backing seam will parallel top and bottom edges of quilt. Baste. Quilt as marked or as desired.

4. From Fabric I strips, make 6¾ yards of straight-grain binding. See page 22 for instructions on making and applying binding.

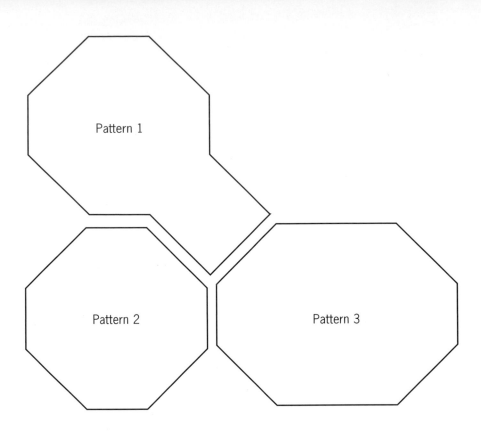

Pattern 1

Pattern 2

Pattern 3

Hanging It Up

Hanging a quilt on the wall adds color and excitement to any decor. But it is important to protect a quilt while showing it off. Only a sturdy, lightweight quilt should be hung. If a quilt is in delicate condition, hanging will only hasten its deterioration.

Making a Hanging Sleeve

The method most often used to hang a quilt is to sew a sleeve on the back so a dowel can be slipped through it. This method distributes the weight evenly across the width of the quilt.

1. From leftover backing fabric, cut or piece an 8"-wide strip that is the same length as the quilt edge.

2. On each end, turn under ½"; then turn under another ½". Topstitch to hem both ends.

3. With wrong sides facing, fold the fabric in half lengthwise and stitch the long edges together. Press seam allowances open and to the middle of the sleeve (Diagram 1).

4. Center the sleeve on the back of the quilt about 1" below the binding with the seam against the backing. Hand-sew the sleeve to the quilt through backing and batting along both long edges.

5. For large quilts, make two or three sleeve sections (Diagram 2) so you can use more nails or brackets to support the dowel to better distribute the quilt's weight.

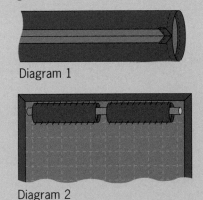

Diagram 1

Diagram 2

Santa Claus *Tree Skirt*

It's easy to put some ho-ho-ho under your tree with this jolly tree skirt. If you have no patience for cutting and sewing lots of little triangles, relax! Quick-piecing takes the trial out of triangles. Stitch, snip, and presto—triangle-squares are ready to go.

Finished Size
Tree Skirt: 53" square
Blocks: 4 santa blocks, 8" x 20"
4 tree blocks, 20" square

Quick-Piecing Techniques
Strip Piecing (see page 12)
Diagonal Corners (see page 12)
Diagonal Ends (see page 13)
Triangle-Squares (see page 14)

Materials

	Fabric I (green print)	2⅛ yards
	Fabric II (parchment solid)	2⅛ yards
	Fabric III (burgundy print)	¾ yard
	Fabric IV (red-green-gold plaid)	½ yard
	Fabric V (white-on-muslin print)	½ yard
	Fabric VI (black solid)	⅛ yard
	Fabric VII (brown solid)	¾ yard
	Backing fabric	3⅜ yards
	Batting	72" x 90"

Black fine-tipped fabric marker or two ½" buttons (optional)

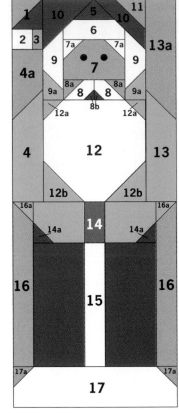

Block A—Make 4.

Cutting
Cut all strips crossgrain, from selvage to selvage. For best use of yardage, cut pieces in order listed. Refer to diagrams to identify pieces.

From Fabric I (green), cut:
* One 18½"-wide strip. From this, cut:
  * One 18½" square for bias binding.
  * Twelve 2" x 18½" strips for outer border.
* Three 9⅛"-wide strips. From these, cut:
  * Five 9⅛" x 18⅝" for B1 triangle-squares.
  * One 8½" square for tree skirt center.
  * Four 3½" squares (B6).
* Two 3½"-wide strips for Strip Set 3.
* Eight 1½"-wide strips. From these, cut:
  * Eight 1½" x 21" (B9).

From Fabric II (parchment), cut:
* Three 9⅛"-wide strips. From these, cut:
  * Five 9⅛" x 18⅝" for B1 triangle-squares.
  * Four 4½" squares (B7).
  * One 4⅜" x 6¾" for A1 triangle-squares.
  * Four 2½" x 3½" (A7).
* Two 7½"-wide strips for Strip Set 3.
* One 6½"-wide strip. From this, cut:
  * Eight 4" x 6½" (B3).
  * Four 2" x 6½" (A13a).
* Two 2"-wide strips. From these, cut:
  * Four 2" x 4" (A4a).
  * Twenty 2" squares (A11, B2).
* Seven 1½"-wide strips. From these and scrap, cut:
  * Eight 1½" x 26" for inner border.
  * Eight 1½" x 8½" (A16).
  * Sixteen 1½" squares (A8a, A17a).
  * Four 1" x 1½" (A3).

From Fabric III (burgundy), cut:
* One 6¾"-wide strip. From this, cut:
  * One 4⅜" x 6¾" for A1 triangle-squares.
  * Two 3" x 37½" strips. From these, cut:
    * Eight 3" squares (A10).
    * Four 1½" x 3½" (A5).
    * Eight 1½" squares (A14a).
* Two 3"-wide strips for Strip Set 2.
* Eight 1"-wide strips. From these, cut:
  * Sixteen 1" x 19" (B8).
  * Eight 1" squares (A8b).

From Fabric IV (plaid), cut:
* Two 3"-wide strips for Strip Set 1.
* One 2½"-wide strip. From this, cut:
  * Eight 2½" squares (A12b).
* One 2"-wide strip. From this and scrap from previous step, cut:
  * Eight 2" x 6" (A4, A13).
* One 1½"-wide strip. From this, cut:
  * Eight 1½" x 2" (A9a).
  * Sixteen 1½" squares (A12a, A16a).

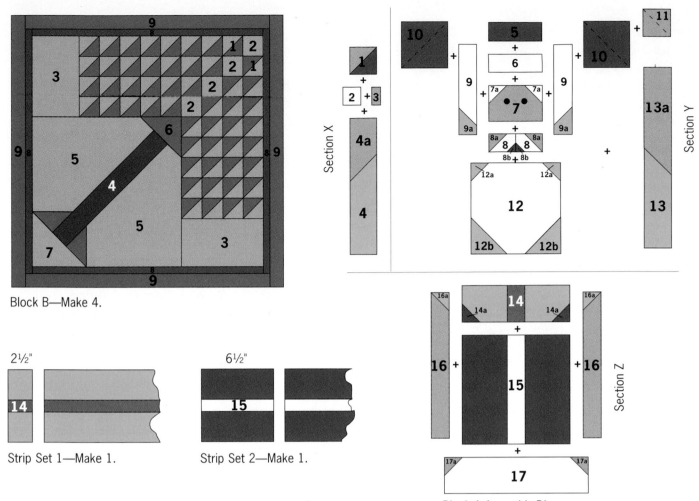

Block B—Make 4.

Section X

Section Y

Section Z

2½"

14

Strip Set 1—Make 1.

6½"

15

Strip Set 2—Make 1.

Block A Assembly Diagram

From Fabric V (white), cut:

✱ One 5½"-wide strip. From this, cut:
  • Four 5½" squares (A12).
  • Four 2½" x 8½" (A17).

✱ Three 1½"-wide strips. Set aside one strip for Strip Set 2. From remaining strips, cut:
  • Twelve 1½" x 3½" (A6, A9).
  • Eight 1½" x 2" (A8).
  • Twelve 1½" squares (A2, A7a).

From Fabric VI (black solid), cut:

✱ One 1½"-wide strip for Strip Set 1.

From Fabric VII (brown solid), cut:

✱ Four 11½" squares (B4).

Units for Block A

Refer to strip set diagrams and Block A Assembly Diagram throughout to identify units.

1. To make Unit 1, see page 14 for instructions on making triangle-squares. On wrong side of 4⅜" x 6¾" piece of Fabric II, draw a 1 x 2-square grid of 2⅜" squares. With right sides facing, align marked fabric with matching piece of Fabric III. Stitch grid as directed on page 14. Cut four triangle-squares from grid, one for each A block.

2. For Strip Set 1, join two 3"-wide strips of Fabric IV and one 1½"-wide strip of Fabric VI as shown. Press seam allowances toward Fabric VI. From this strip set, cut four 2½"-wide segments, one for each A block.

3. For Strip Set 2, join two 3"-wide strips of Fabric III and one 1½"-wide strip of Fabric V as shown. Press seam allowances toward Fabric III. From this strip set, cut four 6½"-wide segments, one for each A block.

4. Use diagonal-corner technique to make two each of units 8 and 16, making mirror-image units as shown. Make one each of units 7, 12, 14, and 17.

5. Use diagonal-end technique to make one each of units 4 and 13. Make two of Unit 9, making one unit a mirror image of the first.

Block A Assembly

Assemble this block in sections X, Y, and Z. Refer to Block A Assembly Diagram throughout.

Section X

1. Join units 2 and 3.
2. Sew Unit 1 to top of 2/3 unit.
3. Sew Unit 4 to bottom to of 2/3 unit as shown. (continued)

Section Y

1. Join two of Unit 8 as shown.
2. Join units 5, 6, 7, and 8.
3. Sew Unit 9 to both sides of row, positioning mirror-image units as shown.
4. Use diagonal-corner technique to sew Unit 10 to both top corners of section.
5. Sew diagonal-corner Unit 11 to top right corner.
6. Sew Unit 12 to bottom of section; then add Unit 13 to right side.

Section Z

1. Join units 14 and 15 as shown.
2. Sew Unit 16 to both sides of 14/15 unit, positioning mirror-image units as shown.
3. Join Unit 17 to bottom of section.

Assembly

Join sections X, Y, and Z to complete block. Make four of Block A.

Block B Assembly

Assemble this block in sections X, Y, and Z. Refer to Block B Assembly Diagram to identify units.

Triangle-Squares

For Unit 1, see page 14 for instructions on making triangle-squares. On wrong side of each 9⅛" x 18⅝" piece of Fabric II, draw a 3 x 7-square grid of 2⅜" squares. With right sides facing, pair each marked fabric with a matching piece of Fabric I. Stitch grids as directed on page 14. Cut 42 triangle-squares from each grid, for a total of 210 (52 for each B block). Discard two.

Section X

1. Select 12 of Unit 1 and four of Unit 2.
2. Join units in four rows, with three of Unit 1 and one Unit 2 in each row. Stagger position of Unit 2 in each row as shown.
3. Join four rows.

Section Y

1. Select 20 of Unit 1 and one Unit 3 for each Section Y.
2. Make four rows of Unit 1, joining five triangle-squares in each row as shown. Join rows.
3. Sew Unit 3 to one end of combined rows as shown.
4. Make two of Section Y.

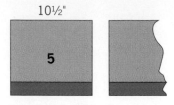

10½"

5

Strip Set 3—Make 2.

Section Z

1. For Strip Set 3, join 7½"-wide strip of Fabric II and 3½"-wide strip of Fabric I as shown (Strip Set 3 Diagram). Make two of Strip Set 3. From these strip sets, cut eight 10½"-wide segments for Unit 5.
2. With right sides facing, position one Unit 5 on top of Unit 4 as shown, matching top left corners (Section Z Diagram, Figure A). Using diagonal-corner technique, stitch from corner to corner of Unit 5.

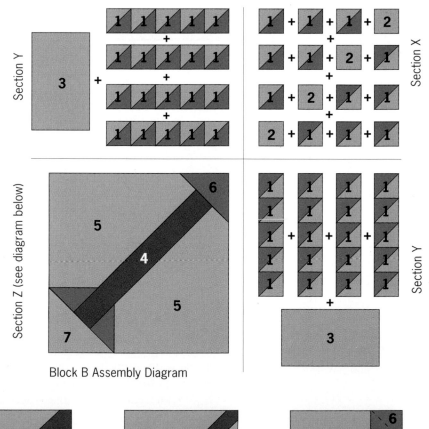

Block B Assembly Diagram

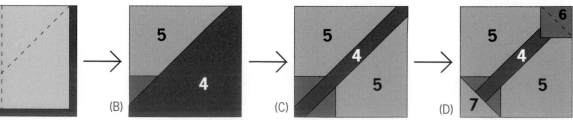

Section Z Diagram

Press Unit 5 to right side (Figure B) and trim excess fabric from seam allowances.

3. Use another strip-set segment to sew another diagonal corner to Unit 4 as shown (Figure C).

4. Use diagonal-corner technique to sew units 6 and 7 to opposite corners as shown (Figure D).

Assembly

1. Join Section Y to left side of Section X as shown.

2. Sew second Section Y to right side of Section Z as shown.

3. Join X/Y section to Y/Z section.

4. Sew a Unit 8 to top and bottom edges of block. Trim ends even with block sides. Then sew a Unit 8 to each side of block. Press seam allowances toward Unit 8.

5. Add Unit 9 to block edges in same manner.

6. Make four of Block B.

Tree Skirt Assembly

1. Referring to photo, sew B blocks to sides of two A blocks.

2. Join two remaining A blocks to sides of 8½" center square.

3. Sew two A/B rows to opposite sides of center row.

Borders

1. For each inner border, join two 1½" x 26" strips of Fabric II.

2. Referring to instructions on page 17, measure quilt from top to bottom. Measuring from center seam, trim two borders to match length. Matching centers, sew borders to quilt sides.

3. Measure quilt from side to side; then trim remaining borders to match quilt width. Sew borders to top and bottom edges. Press seam allowances toward border.

4. For each outer border, join three 2" x 18½" strips of Fabric I end-to-end. Follow steps 2 and 3 to sew borders to tree skirt.

Quilting and Finishing

1. Mark quilting design on tree skirt as desired. Tree skirt shown is outline-quilted.

2. Divide backing into two equal lengths. Cut one piece in half lengthwise. Discard one narrow panel. Join remaining narrow panel to one side of wide piece.

3. Layer backing, batting, and quilt top. Baste. Quilt as desired.

4. Draw a 6" circle in center square. Cut out circle. Referring to photo, cut from circle to one corner of center square. Then cut straight down to edge of tree skirt, cutting through border of Block B.

5. For bias binding, cut 18" square of Fabric I in half diagonally. Starting from cut edges, cut 2"-wide diagonal strips. Join strips end-to-end to make a continuous strip 7 yards long.

6. With wrong sides facing, press binding strip in half. See page 22 for instructions on applying binding. Bias binding should curve nicely around circle.

7. Add eyes to Santas if desired. Use permanent marker to draw eyes or sew on ½"-diameter buttons.

Breezing By

Use scrap fabrics to create a rainbow of hot-air balloons afloat against a sky-blue background. Tassels, braid, and other trims add to the fun of making every block different.

Finished Size

Quilt: 64" x 104"
Blocks: 12 balloon blocks, 14" x 21½"

Materials

▨	Fabric I (light blue solid)	4⅝ yards
▢	Fabric II (yellow solid)	2⅜ yards
▢	Fabric III (assorted scrap fabrics)	scraps
▨	Fabric IV (brown print)	⅛ yard
	Backing fabric	6 yards
	Batting	90" x 108"
	Assorted ribbon, braid, and tassels	scraps
	Brown embroidery floss	

Quick-Piecing Techniques

Strip Piecing (see page 12)
Diagonal Corners (see page 12)
Triangle-Squares (see page 14)
Four-Triangle Squares (see page 15)

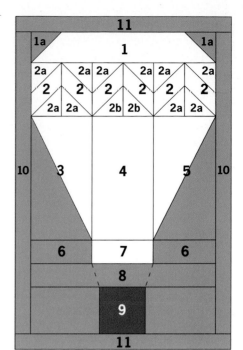

Block A—Make 7.

Cutting

Cut all strips crossgrain, from selvage to selvage. For best use of yardage, cut pieces in order listed. Refer to diagrams to identify pieces.

From Fabric I (light blue), cut:

✱ Four 14½"-wide strips. From these, cut:
- Twelve 11" x 14½" (spacer blocks).
- Twenty-four 1½" x 14½" (A11, B11).

✱ Four 12½"-wide strips. From these, cut:
- Four 12½" x 28¼" for C2 four-triangle squares.
- Twelve 2" x 12½" (A8, B8).
- One 7" x 11¾" for C1 triangle-squares.
- Twenty-four 2½" squares (A1a, B1a).

✱ Two 9⅜"-wide strips. From these, cut:
- Six 9⅜" squares. Cut squares as shown (Diagram 1) to get 12 triangles (A3, B3) and 12 mirror-image triangles (A5, B5). Trim ¾" from triangle tips (Diagram 2). Store triangles in separate bags.
- Four 2" x 23" strips. From these and scrap, cut:
  - Twenty-four 2" x 4½" (A6, B6).

✱ Two 5"-wide strips for Strip Set 1.

✱ Twelve 1½" strips. From these, cut:
- Twenty-four 1½" x 20" (A10, B10).

From Fabric II (yellow), cut:

✱ Four 12½"-wide strips. From these, cut:
- Four 12½" x 28¼" for C2 four-triangle squares.
- One 7" x 11¾" for C1 triangle-squares.

✱ Nine 3"-wide strips for binding.

(continued)

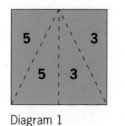

Block B—Make 5.

Diagram 1   Diagram 2

From Fabric III (scraps), cut:

Note: Requirements are listed for one block. Referring to photo, make blocks with as many fabrics as desired.

✱ One 2½" x 12½" (A1).
✱ Six 2½" x 4" (A2).
✱ Ten 2½" squares (A2a).
✱ Two 2½" squares (A2b).
✱ One 9⅜" square. Cut as shown in Diagram 1 to get one each of triangles 3 and 5. Discard extra triangles or use for another block. Trim ¾" from triangle tips (Diagram 2).
✱ One 4½" x 8½" (A4, B4).
✱ One 2" x 4½" (A7, B7).
✱ One 4" x 12½" (B1).
✱ Two 2½" x 4½" (B2).
✱ Six 2½" squares (B2a).
✱ One 2½" x 4½" (B2b).

From Fabric IV (brown), cut:

✱ One 3½"-wide strip for Strip Set 1.

Units for Block A

Refer to Block A Assembly Diagram to identify units. Use scrap fabrics to make one block at a time.

1. Use diagonal-corner technique to make one of Unit 1.

2. For Strip Set 1, join 5"-wide strips of Fabric I and 3½"-wide strip of Fabric IV to make one strip set as shown (Strip Set 1 Diagram). From this, cut twelve 3½"-wide segments for Unit 9. Set aside five units for Block B.

3. For units 3 and 5, join triangles of fabrics I and III as shown.

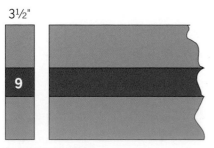

3½"

Strip Set 1—Make 1.

4. For Unit 2, use diagonal-corner technique to make two with 2a corners. Make two mirror-image 2/2a units in same manner but reverse angles of corners. Make one Unit 2 with one 2a corner and one 2b corner as shown. Make one mirror-image 2/2a/2b unit.

Block A Assembly

Assemble this block in sections X and Y. Each completed section should measure approximately 12½" wide. Refer to Block A Assembly Diagram throughout.

1. For Section X, join six of Unit 2 in a row as shown, turning units to get correct fabric placement. Sew Unit 1 to top of row.

2. Join units 3, 4, and 5 in a row.

3. Join units 6 and 7 as shown. Sew this to bottom of 3/4/5 unit.

4. Add units 8 and 9 to bottom of section as shown.

5. Join sections X and Y.

6. Sew Unit 10 to sides of block.

7. Join Unit 11 to top and bottom of block.

8. Make seven of Block A.

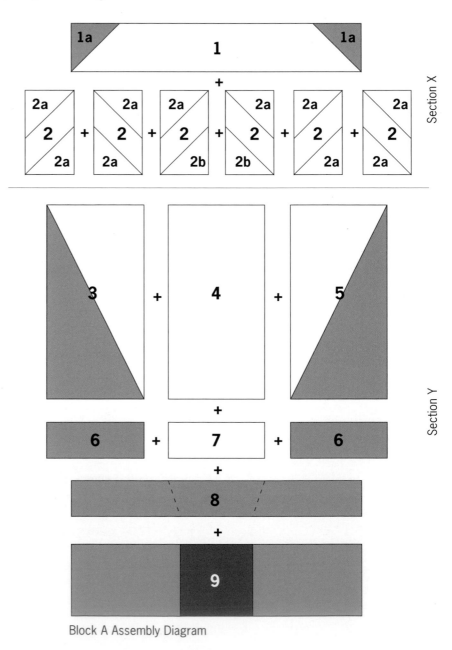

Block A Assembly Diagram

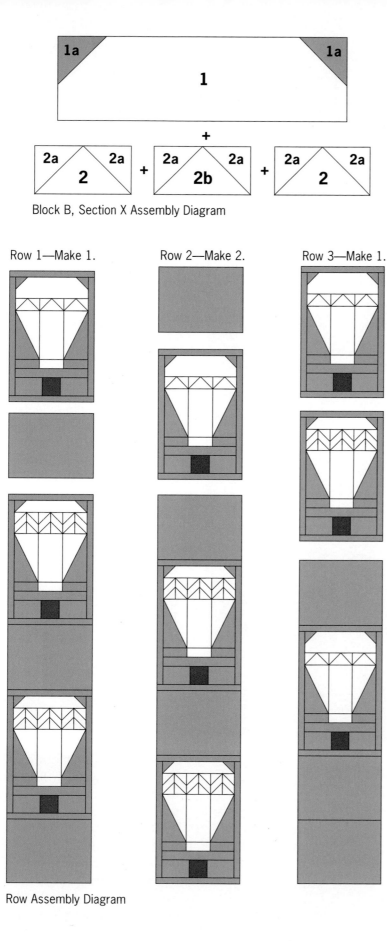

Block B, Section X Assembly Diagram

Row 1—Make 1. Row 2—Make 2. Row 3—Make 1.

Row Assembly Diagram

Block B Assembly

1. Make units 1, 3, and 5 as for Block A.

2. Use diagonal-corner technique to make two of Unit 2/2a as shown. Make one of Unit 2b/2a.

3. Join three of Unit 2 in a row (Block B, Section X Assembly Diagram). Sew Unit 1 to top of row to complete Section X.

4. Follow Block A assembly instructions to complete Block B.

5. Make five of Block B.

Quilt Assembly

1. Referring to photo on page 140 and Row Assembly Diagram, arrange blocks and spacer blocks in rows as shown. Make one each of rows 1 and 3 and two of Row 2. Arrange rows in 1-2-3-2 sequence. Move blocks around to get a pleasing balance of fabrics and color.

2. When satisfied with placement, join blocks in each row.

3. Join rows.

Border

See page 14 for instructions for triangle-squares and four-triangle squares.

1. On wrong side of each 12½" x 28¼" piece of Fabric II, draw a 2 x 5-square grid of 5¼" squares. With right sides facing, pair marked fabric with matching piece of Fabric I. Stitch grids. Cut 20 triangle-squares from each grid to get 76 triangle-squares (and four extra). Press seam allowances toward Fabric I.

2. Draw a diagonal line on wrong side of 38 triangle-squares. With right sides together, match marked triangle-squares with unmarked triangle-squares with opposite fabrics facing. Stitch on both sides of drawn line as directed on page 15. Cut and press to get 76 C2 four-triangle squares. *(continued)*

Border Diagram

3. On wrong side of 7" x 11¾" piece of Fabric II, draw a 1 x 2-square grid of 4⅞" squares. With right sides facing, pair marked fabric with matching piece of Fabric I. Stitch grid. Cut four C1 triangle-squares for border corners.

4. For each side border, join 24 C2 four-triangle squares (Border Diagram). Sew borders to quilt sides, easing as necessary.

5. For top border, join 14 C2 four-triangle squares. Join a C1 square to both ends of border, matching Fabric II edges. Sew border to top edge of quilt. Repeat for bottom border.

Quilting and Finishing

1. Mark quilting design on quilt top as desired. On quilt shown, patchwork is outline-quilted and free-form clouds are quilted in spacer blocks.

2. Divide backing into three 2-yard lengths. Join three panels side-by-side to assemble backing 72" wide.

3. Layer backing, batting, and quilt top. Backing seams will be parallel to top and bottom edges of quilt top. Baste. Quilt as desired.

4. Use two strands of embroidery floss to backstitch lines between balloons and baskets.

5. From Fabric II strips, make 9⅝ yards of straight-grain binding. See page 22 for instructions on making and applying binding.

6. Hand-stitch trims and tassels to balloons as desired.

Cabin in the **Stars**

*Set Log Cabin blocks inside a Variable Star, and you get
a new twist on an old favorite. The three blocks within the block
go together easily with a little piecing secret called a partial seam.*

Finished Size

Quilt: 52" square
Blocks: 4 blocks, 17½" square

Materials

■	Fabric I (black dot)	2 yards
■	Fabric II (gray solid)	½ yard
□	Fabric III (yellow solid)	½ yard
■	Fabric IV (turquoise print)	1 yard
■	Fabric V (magenta solid)	¾ yard
	Fabric VI (magenta print)	½ yard
	Backing fabric	3¼ yards
	Batting	72" x 90"

Quick-Piecing Techniques

Strip Piecing (see page 12)
Diagonal Corners (see page 12)

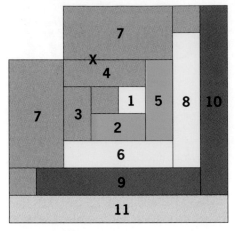

Block A—Make 16.

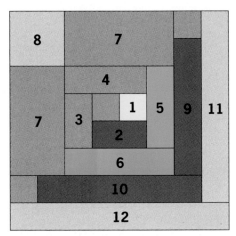

Block B—Make 16.

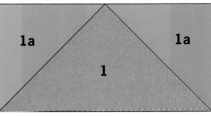

Block C—Make 16.

Cutting

Cut all strips crossgrain, from selvage to selvage, except as noted. For best use of yardage, cut pieces in order listed. Refer to block diagrams to identify pieces.

From Fabric I (black), cut:

✷ Four 1½"-wide strips for Strip Set 5.
✷ Five 1⅛"-wide strips. Set aside two strips for strip sets 1 and 2. From remaining strips, cut:
  • Two 1⅛" x 20" for strip sets 3 and 4.
  • Thirty-two 1⅛" x 1¾" (A3, B3).
✷ Six 3" x 56" lengthwise strips. Set aside four strips for binding. From remaining strips, cut:
  • Sixty-four 1¾" x 3" (A7, B7).
✷ Four 2½" x 56" lengthwise strips for outer border.
✷ Three 4¼" x 56" lengthwise strips. From these, cut:
  • Sixteen 4¼" x 8" (C1).
  • Four 2" squares (inner border corners).
  • Thirty-two 1⅛" x 2⅜" (A4, B4).

From Fabric II (gray), cut:

✷ Two 2½"-wide strips for Strip Set 5.
✷ One 1¾"-wide strip. From this, cut:
  • Sixteen 1¾" squares (B8).
✷ Seven 1⅛"-wide strips. From these, cut:
  • Thirty-two 1⅛" x 5½" (A11, B12).
  • Sixteen 1⅛" x 4⅞" (B11).

From Fabric III (yellow), cut:

✷ One 3⅝"-wide strip. From this, cut:
  • One 3⅝" x 20" for Strip Set 3.
  • Sixteen 1⅛" x 3" (A6).
✷ Five 1½"-wide strips for second border.
✷ One 1⅛"-wide strip for Strip Set 1.

From Fabric IV (turquoise), cut:

✷ Four 4¼"-wide strips. From these, cut:
  • Thirty-two 4¼" squares (C1a).
  • Sixteen 1⅛" x 3" (B6).
✷ Eight 1½"-wide strips. From these, cut:
  • Eight 1½" x 24" for third border.
  • Thirty-two 1⅛" x 2⅜" (A5, B5).
  • Sixteen 1⅛" x 1¾" (A2).

From Fabric V (magenta solid), cut:

✱ One 4¼"-wide strip for Strip Set 2.

✱ One 3⅝" x 20" for Strip Set 4.

✱ Eight 1½"-wide strips. From these, cut:

  • Eight 1½" x 25" for fourth border.

  • Sixteen 1⅛" x 4⅞" (A10).

  • Sixteen 1⅛" x 1¾" (B2).

From Fabric VI (magenta print), cut:

✱ Four 2"-wide strips for inner border.

✱ One 4½" square (center).

Block A Assembly

1. For one Strip Set 1, join 1⅛" strips of fabrics I and III as shown (Strip Set 1 Diagram). From this, cut thirty-two 1⅛"-wide segments for Unit 1. Set aside 16 units for Block B.

2. For one Strip Set 2, join 4¼"-wide strip of Fabric V and 1⅛"-wide strip of Fabric I as shown (Strip Set 2 Diagram). From this, cut thirty-two 1⅛"-wide segments, 16 for A9 and 16 for B10.

3. For Strip Set 3, join 3⅝" x 20" strip of Fabric III and 1⅛" x 20" strip of Fabric I as shown (Strip Set 3 Diagram). From this, cut sixteen 1⅛"-wide segments for Unit 8.

4. Join units 1 and 2 (Diagram 1). Sew Unit 3 to left side of combined units as shown.

5. Working clockwise around block, add units 4, 5, and 6 in numerical order (Diagram 2). As strips are added, press seam allowances away from newest strip.

6. Sew one Unit 7 to left side of block (Diagram 3). With right sides facing, align second Unit 7 with top right corner of block (Unit 5). Stitch seam, stopping about ¾" from end of Unit 4, as shown by X on diagram. Leaving this seam partially open enables you to join blocks A and B without having to sew a set-in seam.

7. Add Unit 8 to right side of block; then sew Unit 9 to bottom edge (Diagram 4). Add units 10 and 11 to complete block.

8. Make 16 of Block A.

Block B Assembly

1. For Strip Set 4, join 3⅝" x 20" strip of Fabric V and 1⅛" x 20" strip of Fabric I as shown (Strip Set 4 Diagram). From this, cut sixteen 1⅛"-wide segments for Unit 9.

(continued)

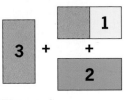

Diagram 1

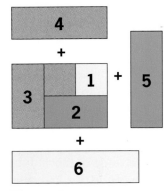

Diagram 2

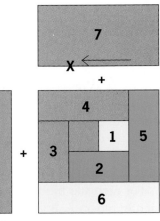

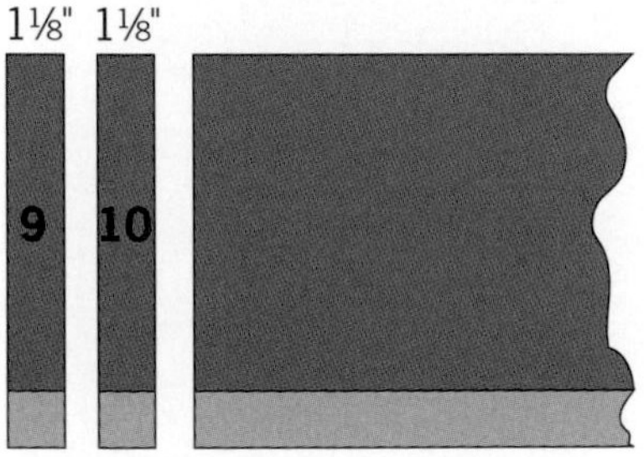

Diagram 3

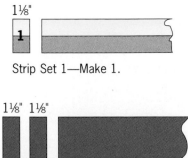

Strip Set 3—Make 1.

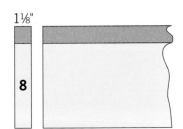

Strip Set 4—Make 1.

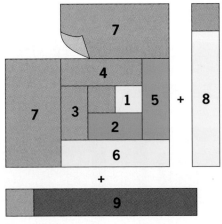

Diagram 4

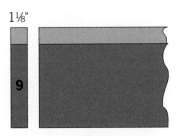

Strip Set 1—Make 1.

Strip Set 2—Make 1.

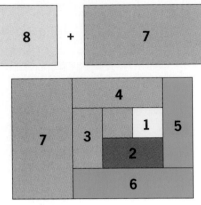

Diagram 5

2. Join units 1–6 in numerical order as for Block A, working clockwise from center and following diagrams for color placement. Add Unit 7 to left side of block. Join Unit 8 to second Unit 7 as shown (Diagram 5); then sew 7/8 unit to top edge of block.

3. Add units 9–12 in same manner as for Block A.

4. Make 16 of Block B.

Block C Assembly

Use diagonal-corner technique to make 16 of Block C.

Star Block Assembly

1. For each star block, select four each of blocks A, B, and C.

2. Join A blocks as shown (Diagram 6), turning blocks to place open corners to outside edges.

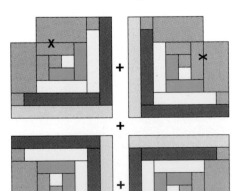

Diagram 6

3. Sew C blocks to edges of joined A blocks as shown (Diagram 7).

4. At one corner of star block, sew a B block to edge indicated by arrow (Diagram 7). Be sure B block is positioned with corner square to inside corner of star block.

5. Starting where partial seam ended, stitch to edge to complete adding Block B.

6. Repeat steps 4 and 5 to join B blocks at remaining corners.

7. Make four star blocks.

Quilt Assembly

1. For Strip Set 5, join two 1½"-wide strips of Fabric I and one

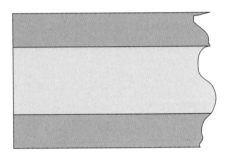

Strip Set 5—Make 2.

2½"-wide strip of Fabric II. Make two strip sets. From these, cut four 18"-long segments for sashing.

2. Referring to photo, join two star blocks with a sashing strip between them. Repeat for second pair of blocks. Press seam allowances toward sashing.

3. For center sashing row, join remaining sashing strips to sides of center square. Press seam allowances toward sashing.

4. Join rows.

Borders

Press seam allowances toward outside edge of quilt throughout.

1. Referring to instructions on page 17, measure quilt from top to bottom and from side to side. Trim Fabric VI border strips to match length.

2. Sew two borders to quilt sides.

3. Add Fabric I squares to ends of remaining borders. Sew borders to top and bottom edges of quilt.

Diagram 7

4. Measure quilt length and piece Fabric III strips as necessary to make two borders. Sew borders to quilt sides. Repeat for top and bottom edges.

5. For third border, join two Fabric IV strips for each border. Measure quilt and sew borders to quilt as before. Repeat for fourth border, using Fabric V border strips.

6. Measure length of quilt again and trim two Fabric I borders to match length. Sew borders to quilt sides. Repeat for top and bottom edges.

Quilting and Finishing

1. Mark quilting design on quilt as desired. Quilt shown is outline-quilted.

2. Divide backing fabric into two equal lengths. Cut one piece in half lengthwise. Join one narrow panel to wide piece. Discard remaining narrow panel.

3. Layer backing, batting, and quilt top. Baste. Quilt as desired.

4. From Fabric I strips, make 6 yards of straight-grain binding. See page 22 for instructions on making and applying binding.

5. See page 130 for tips on making a hanging sleeve.

Nine Lives

Because a cat is a cat, he'll purr at you for hours, and then abruptly turn and show you his south side. Scrap fabrics accentuate the many faces of these quick-pieced kitties. Four little mice prowl the checkerboard borders to make this cat-and-mouse game meowy cute.

Finished Size
Quilt: 80" x 100"
Blocks: 9 cat blocks, 16" x 22"
    4 mouse blocks, 4" x 8"

Materials

	Fabric I (dark blue solid)	3⅛ yards
	Fabric II (light green solid)	1¼ yards
	Fabric III (medium blue solid)	2¼ yards
	Fabric IV (rose solid)	1⅜ yards
	Fabric V (muslin)	¼ yard
	Fabric VI (assorted green, blue, and rose prints)	scraps
	Fabric VII (blue-on-white stripe)	2¼ yards
	Backing fabric	6 yards
	Batting	90" x 108"
	Blue, rose, green, and red yarn	scraps
	Eight ¾"-diameter buttons for cats' eyes	
	Four ½"-diameter buttons for mouse eyes	

Quick-Piecing Techniques
Strip Piecing (see page 12)
Diagonal Corners (see page 12)
Diagonal Ends (see page 13)

Cutting
Cut all strips crossgrain, from selvage to selvage, except as noted. For best use of yardage, cut pieces in order listed.

For scrap fabrics, select three each of blue, green, and rose. In addition to scrap fabrics, use fabrics II, III, and IV for some pieces in blocks A, B, and C. Refer to block diagrams to identify pieces.

From Fabric I (dark blue), cut:
* Six 5½"-wide strips. From these, cut:
  • Eighteen 5½" x 12½" (A1, B1).
* Sixteen 2½"-wide strips. From these and scrap, cut:
  • Eighteen 2½" x 16½" (A11, B10).
  • Twenty-seven 2½" x 6½" (A3, A4, B3, B4).
  • Eighty-four 2½" squares (A2a, A5a, A6a, A7a, B2a, B5a, B6a, C1a, C5).
* One 1½"-wide strip. From this, cut:
  • Four 1½" x 6½" (C3).
  • Eight 1½" squares (B11, C2a).
* Nine 3"-wide strips for binding.

From Fabric II (green), cut:
* One 6½"-wide strip. From this, cut:
  • One 5½" x 6½" (A5).
  • Six 3½" x 6½" (A2, B2).
  • One 4½" x 5½" (A7).
  • Two 4½" squares (A8, Unit D).
* Six 4½"-wide strips for strip sets 2 and 3.
* One 2½"-wide strip. From this, cut:
  • One 2½" x 7½" (A6).
  • Two 2½" x 5½" (B9).
  • Six 2½" squares (A4a, A6c, A10, C4). *(continued)*

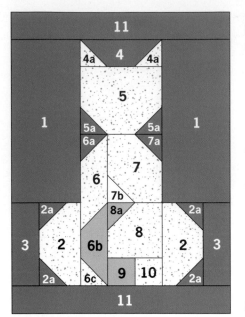

Block A—Make 5.

From Fabric III (medium blue), cut:

* One 6½"-wide strip. From this, cut:
  * One 5½" x 6½" (A5).
  * Two 3½" x 6½" (A2).
  * Two 2½" x 6½" (A6b).
  * One 4½" x 5½" (A7).
  * One 4½" square (A8).
  * One 2½" x 7½" (A6).
  * Eight 2½" squares (A4a, A6c, A8a, A9, A10).
* Fourteen 4½"-wide strips for strip sets 1, 2, and 3.

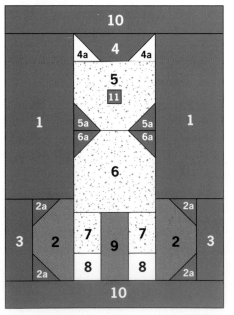

Block B—Make 4.

From Fabric IV (rose), cut:

* One 6½"-wide strip. From this, cut:
  * One 5½" x 6½" (A5).
  * Six 3½" x 6½" (A2, B2). ✓
  * One 4½" x 5½" (A7).
  * One 4½" square (A8).
* Seven 4½"-wide strips for strip sets 1 and 2.
* One 2½"-wide strip. From this, cut:
  * One 2½" x 7½" (A6).
  * Two 2½" x 5½" (B9). ✓
  * Six 2½" squares (A4a, A6c, A10, C4).

From Fabric V (muslin), cut:

* Three 2½"-wide strips. From these, cut:
  * Four 2½" x 8½" (C1).
  * Twenty-one 2½" squares (A7b, B4a, B8).
  * Four 1½" x 6½" (C2).

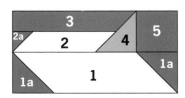

Block C—Make 4.

From Fabric VI (scraps), cut:

* Block A tail pieces from one fabric of each color:
  * One 2½" x 6½" (A6b).
  * Two 2½" squares (A8a, A9).
* Block A body pieces from each of two blue prints:
  * One 5½" x 6½" (A5)
  * One 4½" x 5½" (A7)
  * One 4½" square (A8).
  * Two 3½" x 6½" (A2).
  * One 2½" x 7½" (A6).
  * Four 2½" squares (A4a, A6c, A10).
* Block B body pieces from each of two green and two rose prints:
  * One 6½" square (B6).
  * One 5½" x 6½" (B5).
  * Two 2½" x 3½" (B7).

From Fabric VII (stripe), cut:

* Four 2½" x 77" lengthwise strips for sashing.
* Twelve 3" x 16½" crosswise strips for sashing.

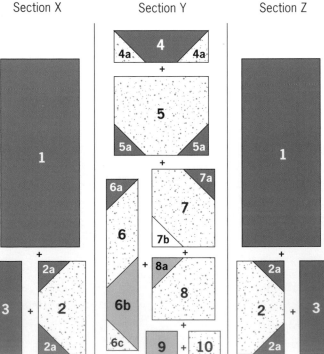

Block A Assembly Diagram

Units for Block A

Refer to Block A Assembly Diagram to identify units.

1. Use diagonal-corner technique to make two of Unit 2 and one each of units 4, 5, 7, and 8.

2. For Unit 6, use diagonal-end technique to join pieces 6 and 6b. Then add diagonal corners to both ends of unit as shown.

Block A Assembly

Assemble this block in sections X, Y, and Z. Each completed section should measure approximately 22½" long. Refer to Block A Assembly Diagram throughout.

Sections X and Z

1. For each section, join units 2 and 3, turning Unit 2s as shown.

2. Add Unit 1 to top of 2/3 units.

Section Y

1. Join units 9 and 10. Sew 9/10 unit to bottom of Unit 8.

2. Sew Unit 7 to top of Unit 8.

3. Join Unit 6 to side of combined unit 7/8/9/10.

4. Sew units 4 and 5 to top of section.

Assembly

1. Sew sections X and Z to sides of Section Y.

2. Join Unit 11 to top and bottom of block.

3. Make five of Block A, using scrap fabrics as shown.

Block B Assembly

Assemble this block in sections X, Y, and Z. Each completed section should measure approximately 22½" long. Refer to Block B Assembly Diagram throughout.

1. Use diagonal-corner technique to make two of Unit 2 and one each of units 4, 5, and 6.

2. For Section X, join units 2 and 3 as shown; then add Unit 1 to top of 2/3 unit.

3. Make Section Z in same manner, turning Unit 2 as shown.

4. For Section Y, join units 7 and 8 in pairs as shown. Sew these to sides of Unit 9. Join units 4, 5, 6, and 7/8/9 in a row as shown.

5. Sew sections X and Z to sides of Section Y.

6. Join Unit 10 to top and bottom of block.

7. Turn under ¼" on all edges of Unit 11. Appliqué square in center of Unit 5.

8. Make four of Block B, using scrap fabrics as shown.

9. Lightly trace smile pattern under each appliquéd nose.

Block C Assembly

Refer to Block C Assembly Diagram to identify units.

1. Use diagonal-corner technique to make one each of units 1 and 2.

2. Join units 2 and 3. Use diagonal-corner technique to add Unit 4 on right side of 2/3 unit as shown.

3. Sew Unit 5 to end of 2/3/4 unit.

4. Sew Unit 1 to bottom of combined unit to complete block.

5. Make four of Block C, making two blocks with Fabric II ears and two blocks with Fabric IV ears.

(continued)

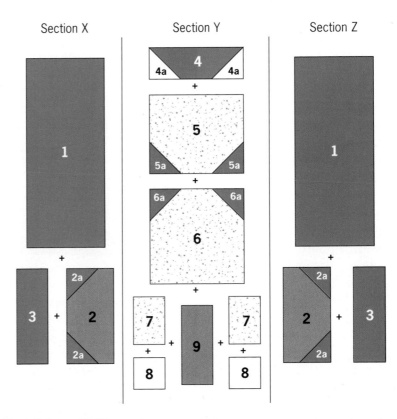

Block B Assembly Diagram

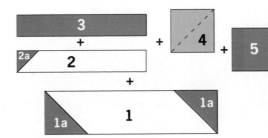

Block C Assembly Diagram

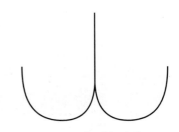

Smile Pattern for Block B

Quilt Assembly

1. Referring to photo, lay out cat blocks in three vertical rows, alternating A and B blocks. Note that blue, rose, and green blocks are set in diagonal lines across the quilt. Place 16½"-long sashing strips between blocks and at top and bottom of each row. When satisfied with block positions, join blocks and sashing strips in each row.

2. Lay out rows again to check position. Place long sashing strips between rows and at both sides. Join rows and sashing.

Border

Refer to quilt photo throughout to check position of units.

1. For Strip Set 1, join two 4½"-wide strips of Fabric III and one strip of Fabric IV as shown (Strip Set 1 Diagram). Press seam allowances toward Fabric III. Make three strip sets. From these, cut twenty-three 4½"-wide segments for Unit 1.

2. For Strip Set 2, join one 4½"-wide strips of Fabrics II, III, and IV as shown (Strip Set 2 Diagram). Press seam allowances toward Fabric III. Make four strip sets. From these, cut thirty-six 4½"-wide segments for Unit 2.

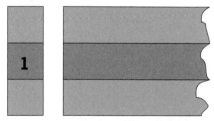

4½"

Strip Set 1—Make 3.

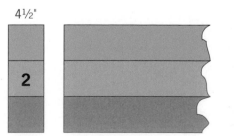

4½"

Strip Set 2—Make 4.

3. For Strip Set 3, join two 4½"-wide strips of Fabric III and one strip of Fabric II as shown. Press seam allowances toward Fabric III. Make two strip sets. From these, cut eighteen 4½"-wide segments for Unit 3.

4. For Unit D, select one Strip Set 2 segment and two Strip Set 3

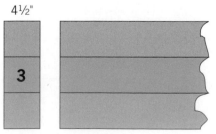

4½"

Strip Set 3—Make 2.

segments. Use a seam ripper to remove one square from each unit, leaving squares of fabrics II and III. Join one discarded square of Fabric III and 4½" square of Fabric II to make a fourth Unit D.

5. For Unit E, remove one Fabric III square from four Strip Set 1 segments.

6. For left side border, select five Unit 1, nine Unit 2, three Unit 3, and one each of Block C, Unit D, and Unit E. Join D and E units to Block C as shown (Left Side Border Diagram). Lay out units in a row, being careful to alternate position of Unit 2 as shown. Join units in row. Sew border to left edge of quilt, positioning bottom of mouse toward outside edge of quilt.

7. For right side border, select five Unit 1, eight Unit 2, four Unit 3, and one each of Block C, Unit D, and Unit E. Join D and E units to Block C as shown (Right Side Border Diagram). Lay out units in a row, being careful to alternate position of Unit 2 as shown. Join units in row. Sew border to right edge of quilt, with bottom of mouse toward outside edge of quilt.

8. For top border, select five Unit 1, nine Unit 2, four Unit 3, and one each of Block C, Unit D, and Unit E. Join D and E units to Block C as shown (Top Border Diagram). Join units in a row as shown. Sew

border to top edge of quilt, with bottom of mouse toward outside edge of quilt.

9. For bottom border, select four Unit 1, nine Unit 2, five Unit 3, and one each of Block C, Unit D, and Unit E. Join D and E units to Block C as shown (Bottom Border Diagram). Join units in a row as shown. Sew border to bottom edge of quilt, with bottom of mouse toward outside edge of quilt.

Quilting and Finishing

1. Mark quilting design on quilt top as desired. On quilt shown, patchwork is outline-quilted. The background of each block is machine stipple-quilted.

2. Divide backing into two 3-yard lengths. Cut one piece in half lengthwise. Join one narrow panel to each side of wide piece to assemble backing.

3. Layer backing, batting, and quilt top. Baste. Quilt as marked or as desired.

4. From Fabric I strips, make 10½ yards of straight-grain binding. See page 22 for instructions on making and applying binding.

5. Sew two ¾" buttons on each B block for cats' eyes. Sew a ½" button in place on each C block.

6. Use yarn scraps to backstitch mouths and whiskers on cats and a tail for each mouse. On B blocks, tack a long length of yarn on each side of cat's neck and tie a bow.

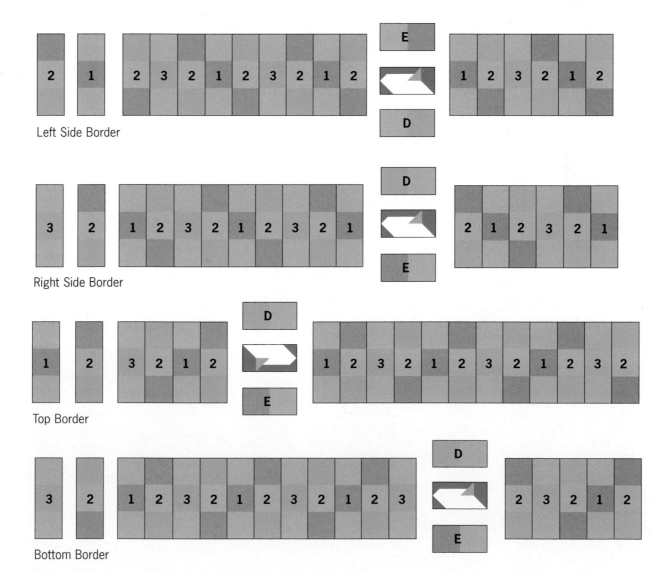

Left Side Border

Right Side Border

Top Border

Bottom Border

Don't Sit Under the **Apple Tree**

You'll be humming the familiar tune as you stitch this orchard of apple trees. The cheery picnic cloth also features falling apples and an army of happy ants ready for the feast to begin. Strip piecing makes the trees and checkerboard border extra quick.

Finished Size

Picnic Cloth: 60" x 60"
Blocks: 8 tree blocks, 13¾" square
12 ant blocks, 2½" x 13¾"

Quick-Piecing Techniques

Strip Piecing (see page 12)
Diagonal Corners (see page 12)

Materials

■	Fabric I (red print)	1⅝ yards
□	Fabric II (white-on-white print)	2 yards
▨	Fabric III (lime green print)	¼ yard
▨	Fabric IV (dark green print)	⅞ yard
■	Fabric V (brown print)	⅝ yard
▨	Fabric VI (bright blue solid)	⅝ yard
	Backing fabric	3⅞ yards
	Batting	72" x 90"
	Brown fine-tipped fabric marker	

Cutting

Cut all strips crossgrain, from selvage to selvage, except as noted. For best use of yardage, cut pieces in order listed. Refer to block diagrams to identify pieces. See page 125 for tips on cutting appliqué pieces with freezer paper.

From Fabric I (red), cut:

✳ Eighteen 1¾"-wide strips. Set aside 16 strips for strip sets 1 and 2. From two strips, cut:
  • Thirty-two 1¾" squares (A6, sashing squares).
✳ Eight apples for appliqué.
✳ Six 3"-wide strips for binding.

Apple Pattern

From Fabric II (white), cut:

✳ One 14¼"-wide strip. From this, cut:
  • One 14¼" square (center square).
  • Sixteen 1⅛" x 14¼" (A12).
✳ Two 6¾"-wide strips. From these and scrap, cut:
  • Sixteen 5½" x 6¾" (A10).
✳ Three 3"-wide strips. From these, cut:
  • Sixteen 3" x 6¾" (A7).
  • Four 3" squares (Corner C).
✳ Four 1¾"-wide strips. From these and scrap, cut:
  • Sixteen 1¾" x 4¼" (A9).
  • Sixteen 1¾" x 3" (A3).
  • Thirty-two 1¾" squares (A4, A8a).
✳ Five 1½"-wide strips. From these, cut:
  • Twelve 1½" x 14¼" (B6).
  • Twelve 1¼" x 1½" (B4).
  • Twenty-four 1" x 1½" (B3).

From Fabric II (white), cut: [continued column 3]

✳ Eleven 1"-wide strips. From these, cut:
  • Twelve 1" x 14¼" (B5).
  • 288 1" squares (B1a, B2a).

From Fabric III (lime green), cut:

✳ Five 1¾"-wide strips for Strip Set 2. *(continued)*

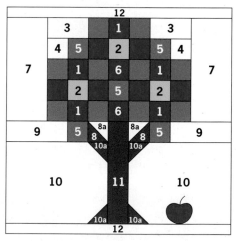

Block A—Make 8.

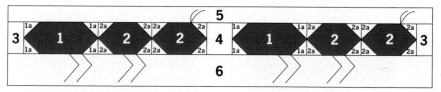

Block B—Make 12.

From Fabric IV (dark green), cut:

✱ Fourteen 1¾"-wide strips. Set aside 12 strips for Strip Set 1. From two strips, cut:
- Forty 1¾" squares (A5).

From Fabric V (brown), cut:

✱ Four 1¾"-wide strips. From these, cut:
- Eight 1¾" x 6¾" (A11).
- Forty-eight 1¾" squares (A8, A10a).

✱ Five 1½"-wide strips. From these, cut:
- Twenty-four 1½" x 3" (B1).
- Forty-eight 1½" x 2¼" (B2).

From Fabric VI (blue), cut:

✱ Ten 1¾"-wide strips. From these, cut:
- Twenty-four 1¾" x 14¼" (E sashing).
- Sixteen 1¾" x 3" (D sashing).

Units for Block A

Refer to strip set diagrams and Block A Assembly Diagram to identify units.

1. For Strip Set 1, join 1¾"-wide strips of fabrics I and IV as shown. Make six strip sets. Press seam allowances toward Fabric IV. From these strip sets, cut 128 1¾"-wide segments for Unit 1. Set aside 88 units for border.

2. For Strip Set 2, join 1¾"-wide strips of fabrics I and III as shown. Make five strip sets. Press seam allowances toward Fabric III. From these strip sets, cut 112 1¾"-wide segments for Unit 2. Set aside 88 units for border.

3. Use diagonal-corner technique to make two of Unit 10.

4. For Unit 8, match 1¾" squares of fabrics II and V, with right sides facing. On wrong side of Fabric II square, draw one diagonal line from corner to corner. Stitch on diagonal line. Trim seam allowance to ¼" and press. Make 16 of Unit 8, two for each block.

Block A Assembly

Assemble block in sections X and Y. Completed sections should be 14¼" wide. Refer to Block A Assembly Diagram throughout.

Section X

Main part of section consists of five horizontal rows as shown.

1. Join a Unit 3 to sides of Unit 1.

2. Join units 4 and 5 to sides of Unit 2.

3. Sew Unit 1s to sides of Unit 6. Repeat to make Row 5.

4. Join Unit 2s to opposite sides of one Unit 5.

5. Join rows 1–5.

6. Sew Unit 7s to sides of combined rows.

Section Y

1. Join units 5, 8, and 9, making two mirror-image rows as shown.

2. Sew each 5/8/9 row to top of one Unit 10.

3. Sew combined units to sides of Unit 11.

Assembly

1. Join sections X and Y.

2. Stitch Unit 12 to top and bottom of block.

3. Make 8 of Block A.

4. Appliqué apples at Unit 12 seam line. Use fabric pen to draw stems.

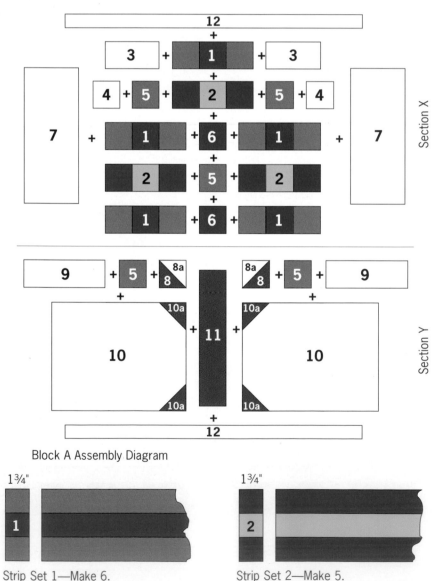

Block A Assembly Diagram

Strip Set 1—Make 6.

Strip Set 2—Make 5.

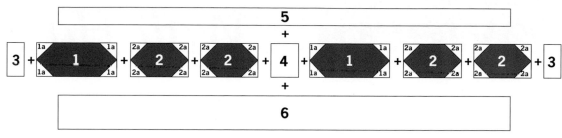

Block B Assembly Diagram

Block B Assembly

Each completed block should measure 14¼" wide. Refer to Block B Assembly Diagram throughout.

1. Use diagonal-corner technique to make two of Unit 1 and four of Unit 2.

2. Join units in a row with units 3 and 4 as shown.

3. Sew Unit 5 to top of block and Unit 6 to bottom.

4. Use fabric pen to draw legs and antenna.

Picnic Cloth Assembly

Assemble borders and blocks in horizontal rows. Refer to photo and Row Assembly Diagram throughout.

1. For Border Row, alternate 24 Strip Set 1 units and 23 Strip Set 2 units. Make two Border Rows.

2. For Row 1, join two pair of strip-set units as shown for ends of row. Join these with corner C, four D sashing strips, three B blocks, and another C square as shown. Make two of Row 1.

3. For Row 2, join two Strip Set 2 units, two D sashing strips, three E sashing strips, and four sashing squares. Make four of Row 2.

4. For Row 3, join three A blocks, four E sashing strips, and two B blocks as shown. For both ends of row, join six Strip Set 1 units and five Strip Set 2 units as shown; then sew these to row. Make two of Row 3.

5. For Row 4, join two A blocks, center square, two B blocks, and four E sashing strips as shown. For both ends of row, join six Strip Set 1 units and five Strip Set 2 units; then sew these to row. Make one of Row 4.

6. Lay out rows 1-3-4-3-1. Then put a Row 2 between each row. Lay out border rows at top and bottom. When satisfied with position of all rows, join rows.

Quilting and Finishing

1. Mark quilting design on cloth as desired. Cloth shown is outline-quilted.

2. Divide backing into two equal lengths. Cut one panel in half lengthwise and discard one narrow panel. Sew remaining narrow panel to wide panel to assemble backing.

3. Layer backing, batting, and cloth. Baste. Quilt as desired.

4. From Fabric I strips, make 7 yards of binding. See page 22 for directions on making and applying straight-grain binding.

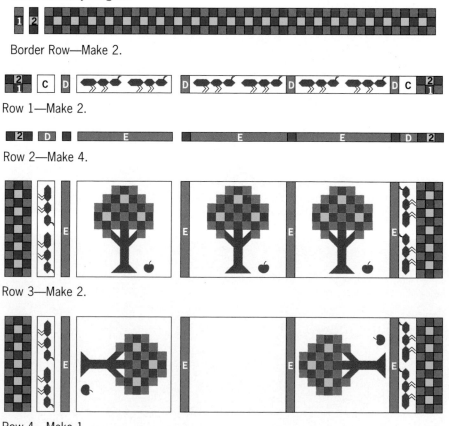

Row Assembly Diagram

Border Row—Make 2.

Row 1—Make 2.

Row 2—Make 4.

Row 3—Make 2.

Row 4—Make 1.

Flowerpot *Wall Hanging*

*Looking for a pretty way to store tools? Make this little wall hanging
for your sewing room, potting shed, or kitchen. Four handy pockets hold
quilting supplies, small gardening tools, note cards, or just stuff.*

Finished Size

Quilt: 22½" x 29½"
Blocks: 4 flowerpot blocks, 5" x 11"
      4 heart pocket blocks, 2½" x 6"

Materials

■	Fabric I (blue print)	⅜ yard
▧	Fabric II (dark blue solid)	¼ yard
■	Fabric III (navy solid)	⅝ yard
■	Fabric IV (green solid)	¼ yard
■	Fabric V (terra-cotta solid)	⅛ yard
■	Fabric VI (rust print)	⅛ yard
□	Fabric VII (printed muslin)	½ yard
	Backing fabric	⅞ yard
	Batting	29" x 36"

Four ⅞"-diameter white buttons

Quick-Piecing Techniques

Diagonal Corners (see page 12)
Four-Triangle Squares (see page 15)

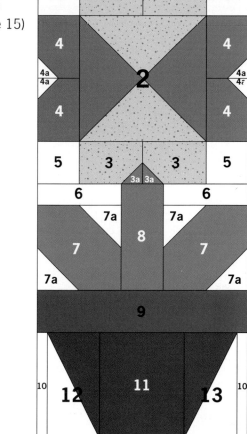

Block A—Make 4.

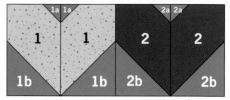

Block B—Make 4.

Cutting

Cut all strips crossgrain, from selvage to selvage. For best use of yardage, cut pieces in order listed. Refer to diagrams to identify pieces.

From Fabric I (blue), cut:

✱ One 6¼"-wide strip. From this, cut:
- One 6¼" x 10½" for A2 triangle-squares.
- Two 2" x 31" strips. From these, cut:
  - Sixteen 1½" x 2" (A1, A3).
  - Eight 2" x 3" (B1).
✱ Three 1¼"-wide strips for inner border.

From Fabric II (dark blue), cut:

✱ One 6¼"-wide strip. From this, cut:
- One 6¼" x 10½" for A2 triangle-squares.
- Sixteen 1½" x 2" (A4).

From Fabric III (navy), cut:

✱ Four 2"-wide strips. From these, cut:
- Two 2" x 27" and two 2" x 23" for outer borders.
- Eight 2" x 3" (B2).
✱ Three 3"-wide strips for binding.

From Fabric IV (green), cut:

✱ One 2½"-wide strip. From this, cut:
- Eight 2½" squares (A7).
- Four 1½" x 3" (A8).
✱ One 2¼" x 24½" (16).
✱ One 2"-wide strip. From this and scrap, cut:
- Sixteen 2" squares (B1b, B2b).
- Twenty-four 1" squares (A3a, B1a, B2a).

From Fabric V (terra-cotta), cut:

✱ Four 1½" x 5½" (A9).

From Fabric VI (rust), cut:

✱ One 3⅞"-wide strip. From this, cut:
- One 3⅞" x 7¾". From this, cut four A12 triangles and four A13 triangles as shown (Diagram 1). Trim ¾" from tip of each triangle (Diagram 2). Store triangles separately.
- Four 2½" x 3" (A11).

(continued)

From Fabric VII (muslin), cut:

✳ One 5½"-wide strip. From this, cut:
- One 5½" x 24½" (17).
- Two 1" x 5½" (18).
- One 3⅞" x 7¾". From this, cut four A12 triangles and four A13 triangles as shown (Diagram 1). Trim ¾" from tip of each triangle (Diagram 2). Store triangles separately.
- Eight ¾" x 3" (A10).

✳ Four 1½"-wide strips. From these, cut:
- Two 1½" x 25½" (15).
- Five 1½" x 11½" (14).
- Thirty-two 1½" squares (A5, A7a).

✳ One 1"-wide strip. From this and scrap, cut:
- Eight 1" x 2½" (A6).
- Twenty-four 1" squares (A1a, A4a).

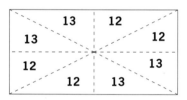

Diagram 1

Diagram 2

Units for Block A

Refer to Block A Assembly Diagram throughout to identify units.

1. On wrong side of 6¼" x 10½" piece of Fabric I, draw a 1 x 2-square grid of 4¼" squares.
2. With right sides facing, match marked piece with corresponding piece of Fabric II. Stitch grid as described for triangle-squares on page 14. Cut four triangle-squares from grid. Press seam allowances toward Fabric II.

3. See page 15 for instructions on four-triangle squares. Draw a diagonal line on wrong side of two triangle-squares. With right sides facing and seams aligned, match a marked triangle-square with unmarked unit so that each triangle faces a different fabric. Stitch each pair as directed on page 15. Make four four-triangle squares for Unit 2, one for each block.
4. Join triangles of fabrics VI and VII to make one each of units 12 and 13.
5. Use diagonal-corner technique to make two each of units 1, 3, and 7 as shown. Note that second unit is mirror image of the first. Make units in same manner, but reverse angles of diagonal corners. Make four of Unit 4 in same manner.

Block A Assembly

Assemble this block in sections X, Y, and Z. Each completed section should measure approximately 5½" wide. Refer to Block A Assembly Diagram throughout.

Section X

1. Join units 1 and 3 in pairs as shown.
2. Sew combined units to top and bottom of Unit 2 as shown.
3. Join two pair of Unit 4, matching mirror-image units as shown. Sew Unit 5 to ends of each pair.
4. Join 4/5 units to sides of 1/2/3 unit.

Section Y

1. Sew Unit 6 to top of each Unit 7.
2. Join 6/7 units to sides of Unit 8.
3. Sew Unit 9 to bottom of section.

Section Z

Join units 10, 11, 12, and 13 in a row as shown.

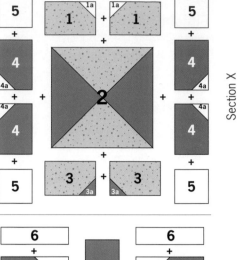

Section X

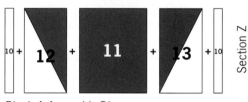

Section Y

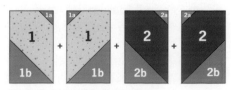

Section Z

Block A Assembly Diagram

Assembly

1. Join sections X, Y, and Z as shown.
2. Make four of Block A.

Block B Assembly

Refer to Block B Assembly Diagram throughout.
1. Use diagonal-corner technique to make one each of units 1 and 2. Second unit is a mirror image of the first.
2. Join units in a row as shown.
3. Make four of Block B.

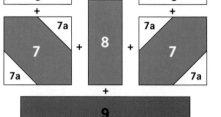

Block B Assembly Diagram

Quilt Assembly

Refer to Quilt Assembly Diagram for placement of blocks and setting pieces in rows.

1. Join A blocks in a row with a Unit 14 strip between blocks and at row ends as shown.

2. Sew Unit 15 to top of row.

3. Join B blocks in a row. Sew Unit 16 to top of row.

4. Turn under ¼" on top edge of Unit 16. Then turn under another ¼" and press. Topstitch fold to make hem for pocket. Pin B/16 to Unit 17, matching sides and bottom edge.

5. Stitch Unit 18 to sides of pocket section, sewing through all layers. Sew Unit 15 to bottom edge in same manner.

6. Join sections.

Borders

1. Referring to instructions on page 17, measure quilt from side to side. Cut two 1¼"-wide Fabric I strips to match width. Sew borders to top and bottom edges of quilt.

2. Measure quilt from top to bottom; then cut two borders from remaining strip to match quilt length. Sew borders to quilt sides.

3. For outer border, measure quilt and trim Fabric III strips to fit. Sew borders to quilt as before.

Quilting and Finishing

1. Mark quilting design on quilt top as desired. On wall hanging shown, patchwork is outline-quilted.

2. Cut a 29" x 36" piece of backing fabric. Layer backing, batting, and quilt top. Baste. Quilt as marked or as desired. Topstitch through all layers between B blocks to top of Unit 16 to make four pockets.

3. Sew buttons to flower centers.

4. From Fabric III strips, make 3¼ yards of straight-grain binding. See page 22 for instructions on making and applying binding.

5. See page 130 for directions on making a hanging sleeve.

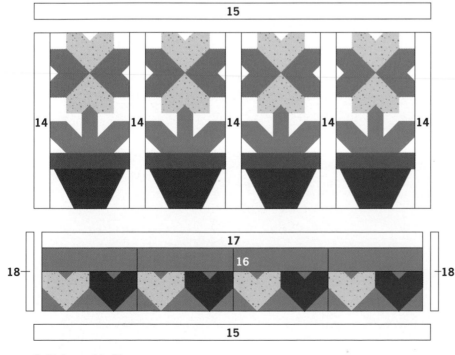

Quilt Assembly Diagram

Design Credits

Baby Buggies Crib Set: Mindy Kettner
Breezing By: Pam Bono
Cabin in the Stars: Robert Bono
Chains of Love: Pam Bono
Counting Sheep: Pam and Robert Bono
Crows in the Corn: Mindy Kettner
Don't Sit Under the Apple Tree: Mindy Kettner
Field of Flowers: Pam Bono
Field of Flowers Wall Hanging: Pam Bono
Flowerpot Wall Hanging: Mindy Kettner
Flowers in the Cabin: Pam and Robert Bono
Flying Home: Mindy Kettner
Grandmother's Violets: Pam Bono, Robert Bono,
  Mindy Kettner
Intersection: Robert Bono
It's Okay to Be Different: Mindy Kettner
Keep On Truckin': Mindy Kettner
Nine Lives: Mindy Kettner
Old Bones: Pam Bono, Dallas Bono, Mindy Kettner
Pinwheels: Pam and Robert Bono
Primrose: Pam Bono
Santa Claus Tree Skirt: Pam Bono
Sunflowers: Pam Bono, Robert Bono, Mindy Kettner
Sweet Dreams: Mindy Kettner
Tea for Two: Mindy Kettner

Quilting Credits

Baby Buggies Crib Set and *Flowerpot Wall Hanging:*
  Mindy Kettner
Breezing By, Crows in the Corn, It's Okay to Be Different,
  and *Keep On Truckin':* Wanda Nelson of Knit One,
  Quilt Too
Cabin in the Stars: Ella Ross
Chains of Love, Counting Sheep, Intersection, Nine Lives,
  Old Bones, Pinwheels, and *Sweet Dreams:* Julie Tebay of
  Quilting Plus
Field of Flowers Wall Hanging: Marguleta Westbrook and
  Elizabeth Smith
Field of Flowers, Flowers in the Cabin, Flying Home,
  Grandmother's Violets, Primrose, Santa Claus Tree Skirt,
  and *Sunflowers:* Amish hand quilting by Quilting Plus

Photography Credits

All photographs by **John O'Hagan** except the
  following:
James Boone: cover landscape photo
Keith Harrelson: pages 46, 56, 63, 80, 104, 120, 136,
  152, 156.
Brit Huckaby: pages 41, 68, 73, 92, 98, 146.

Special thanks to:

✱ Wanda Nelson and Charo Nelson of Knit One, Quilt Too in Farmington, New Mexico, for making hanging sleeves and for a very special friendship.

✱ Barbara Morgan of Animas Quilts in Durango, Colorado, for helping with last-minute bindings.

✱ Megan Kettner, Julia Kettner, Wendy Wandio, Carol Harold, Kathrine Jones, and Karen Koch, for helping Mindy with cutting and pressing.

✱ Dorothy Davis for her special button box, as well as for continued friendship and support.

✱ Julie Tebay of Quilting Plus in Rochester, Minnesota, whose wonderful work makes us very grateful to have found her and her Amish quilters. Thanks for meeting deadlines and for taking extra time to make everything beautiful.

✱ The Brass Bed of Homewood, Alabama, for the loan of the bed pictured on the cover.

✱ Bernina of America for the use of a wonderful sewing machine, model 1630.

✱ Dallas and Ryan Bono, our sons, whose understanding and support make our family a great partnership and a fun place to be. We are so proud of your talents.